A Manual
of
Parliamentary
Practice

THOMAS JEFFERSON

NEW YORK

A Manual of Parliamentary Practice
Cover © 2007 Cosimo, Inc.

For information, address:

Cosimo, P.O. Box 416
Old Chelsea Station
New York, NY 10113-0416

or visit our website at:
www.cosimobooks.com

A Manual of Parliamentary Practice was originally published in 1801.

Cover design by www.kerndesign.net

ISBN: 978-1-60206-103-3

TABLE OF CONTENTS

INTRODUCTION

Born in 1743, 250 years before this reprinting of his *A Manual of Parliamentary Practice for the Use of the Senate of the United States*, Thomas Jefferson thought his legacy would be authorship of the Declaration of Independence, founding of the University of Virginia, and writing the Virginia Statute for Religious Freedom, all of which he directed were to be noted on his tombstone. Yet it is a measure of Jefferson's genius that his varied accomplishments beyond these three things are so significant that most individuals would be proud to count any one of them the crowning success of a lifetime. For instance, his architectural plans for Monticello, his mountaintop home near Charlottesville, Virginia; for Poplar Forest, his splendid octagonal retreat in a Palladian style near Lynchburg, Virginia; and for the Virginia state capitol in Richmond, modeled on the Maison Carrée at Nimes, France, which he described as "noble beyond expression," are all studied today for their interpretation of classical designs and admired for their elegance and practicality.

Another example is the library Jefferson

took fifty years forming and which was the largest in America when he sold it to the U.S. Congress in 1815 to replace the Congressional library that had been destroyed by the British during the war of 1812. Jefferson's library became the foundation of the Library of Congress, today the largest library in the world. The 2,700 remaining books of the original Jefferson collection are now housed in the Library's Rare Book and Special Collections Division, where they are still consulted by scholars pursuing an understanding of the Enlightenment in America.

Jefferson served with distinction as a member of the Continental Congress, minister to France for the young republic, Secretary of State, Vice President, and President of the United States in two pivotal terms when the boundaries of the country were dramatically expanded. Throughout his life Jefferson's universal curiosity and systematic search for knowledge led him to investigate numerous aspects of human endeavor and natural phenomena as well, laying the groundwork for a variety of professions in this country. Librarians, landscape architects, educators, nutritionists, enologists, meteorologists, classicists, and horticulturalists are among those who look to Jefferson as a founding father in their fields.

Jefferson's authorship of *A Manual of Parliamentary Practice for the Use of the Senate of the United States* is another example of a milestone in still another area. It is typical of Jefferson's finely organized and persistent mind that the beginnings of the *Manual* can be traced to his student days between 1760 and 1762 at William and Mary College in Williamsburg, Virginia, when as a student of William Small he studied parliamentary law. He later recalled that he read deeply on the subject, and he copied into a notebook passages from his reading that he found particularly compelling.

Not long afterward, Jefferson saw first-hand the adverse effects of a lack of rules and procedures in a legislative body. Observing the Maryland legislature in Annapolis during the Spring of 1766, he wrote of its deliberations: "The mob (for such was their appearance) sat covered on the justices' and lawyers' benches, and were divided into little clubs amusing themselves in the common chit chat way. I was surprised to see them address the speaker without rising from their seats, and three, four, and five at a time without being checked. When [a motion was] made, the speaker instead of putting the question in the usual form only asked the gentlemen whether they chose whether such and such a thing be done, and was answered by a yes sir, or no sir: and tho' the voices appeared frequently to be divided, they would never go to the trouble of dividing the house, but the clerk entered the resolutions, I suppose, as he thought proper. In short everything seems to be carried without the house in general's knowing what was proposed."

Before 1776, the assemblies in each of the American colonies looked to England for procedural guidance, which consisted primarily of rules laid out in the journals of the House of Lords, which began in 1510, and those of the House of Commons, which started in 1547. These procedural rules, however, were not codified in any systematic way. Tradition and memory often altered the written record, and procedures from colony to colony sometimes varied greatly. Moreover, if Jefferson's observations in Annapolis were the norm, even rudimentary rules of deportment and practice were not consistently applied.

Between 1769 and 1779, Jefferson served successively in the Virginia House of Burgesses, the Continental Congress, and the Virginia House of Delegates. Such legislative experience must have enriched his understanding of parliamentary practice and focused his reading as he continued to make entries in his parliamentary commonplace book, which has since been edited by Wilbur Samuel Howell and published with the title *Jefferson's Parliamentary Writings* (Princeton University Press, 1988). In the Continental Congress Jefferson was appointed to a committee of three charged with drawing up rules to guide that body's proceedings. His greatest challenge in parliamentary practice came in 1797 when as vice president of the United States he presided over the Senate. Though frustrated by his inability to affect policy directly unless a tie vote occurred, Jefferson characteristically applied himself with diligence to his role in ensuring orderly debate and decision making. To that end his forty years' worth of notes on parliamentary practice must have been invaluable.

It was Jefferson's original intention to leave his manuscript notes on parliamentary practice to the Senate for future vice presidents, but he later decided to organize the notes and develop them into a manual for publication so that the material would be both easier to use and available to the public. He directed the printer of the first edition to issue it in a small format so that senators could easily carry it onto the floor and consult its contents at appropriate moments, thereby ensuring adherence to the rules. It was published in 1801 in the City of

Washington by Samuel Harrison Smith, editor of the pro-Jefferson newspaper, *The National Intelligencer.*

Among Jefferson's main intents in publishing his *Manual* was to ensure the rights of the minority, an issue that was one of the touchstones of the Revolutionary Age. Jefferson felt that any majority in a legislative body could become as oppressive in its treatment of the rights of others as was King George III of the rights of the American colonists. At the outset of the *Manual* he emphasized the importance of rules protecting the rights of the minority by quoting a former Speaker of the House of Commons: "...nothing tended more to throw power into the hands of administration and those who acted with the majority of the House of Commons, than a neglect of, or departure from, the rules of proceeding: that these forms, as instituted by our ancestors, operated as a check, and control on the actions of the majority, and that they were in many instances, a shelter and protection to the minority, against the attempts of power."

Having set the tone for the book, Jefferson then lays out systematically the ground rules for accepting the qualifications of elected legislators, Congressional privilege, rules for the committee of the whole, the order of debates, the introduction of bills, amendments, decorum, adjournment, and other such matters that are essential for a fair and orderly working of deliberative bodies. The volume is less an original piece of writing than a compilation of the work of previous writers on parliamentary practice, and Jefferson is careful to note the contributions of each. He most frequently relies on *Lex Parliamentaria* by George Peyt, first published in London in 1790, often cited in the text as *Lex Parl*. The next most commonly cited work is John Hatsell's *Precedents of Procedings in the House of Commons* (London, 1785), usually cited *Hats*. A full listing of Jefferson's abbreviations for works cited in the *Manual* can be found in Thais Plaisted's *Thomas Jefferson: Parliamentarian* (Los Angeles, 1978) or in the previously cited *Jefferson's Parliamentary Writings*. Some of the books Jefferson cites date from the sixteenth century.

Though Jefferson intended his *Manual* to be used primarily by the small group of senators, his typical thoroughness and ability to distill the essence of a subject resulted in a book that stirred great interest among citizens everywhere concerned with the correct manner of conducting a meeting. After its publication in 1801, the *Manual* quickly gained the admiration of a wide circle of readers. Translations in French and Spanish were soon issued, and some 150 editions have appeared since the book was first published.

The current edition of the House of Representatives' Rule 42 states: "The rules of parliamentary practice comprised in Jefferson's Manual and the provisions of the Legislative Reorganization Act of 1946, as amended, shall govern the House in all cases to which they are applicable...." Ironically, the Senate, for which the *Manual* was originally intended, no longer uses it, but the House of Representatives consults the *Manual* daily about such matters as amendments, disagreements between the House and the Senate, debate standards, and other basic matters that ensure a fair hearing in the Congress and ultimately a guarantee of liberty in the republic.

> *James Gilreath*
> *American History Specialist*
> *Rare Book and Special*
>   *Collections Division*
> *Library of Congress*

PREFACE

THE Constitution of the United States establishing a legislature for the Union under certain forms, authorises each branch of it 'to determine the rules of its own proceedings.' The Senate have accordingly formed some rules for its own government: but these going only to few cases, they have referred to the decision of their President, without debate and without appeal, all questions of order arising either under their own rules, or where they have provided none. This places under the discretion of the President a very extensive field of decision, and one which, irregularly exercised, would have a powerful effect on the proceedings and determinations of the house. The President must feel weightily and seriously this confidence in his discretion; and the necessity of recurring, for its government, to some known system of rules, that he may neither leave himself free to indulge caprice or passion, nor open to the imputation of them. But to what system of rules is he to recur, as supplementary to be those of the Senate? To this there can be but one answer; to the system of regulations adopted for the government of some one of the parliamentary bodies within these states, or of that which has served as a prototype to most of them. This last is the model which we have all studied; while we are little acquainted with the modifications of it in our several states. It is deposited too in publications possessed by many and open to all. Its rules are probably as wisely constructed for governing the debates of a deliberative body, and obtaining its true sense, as any which can become known to us; and the acquiescence of the Senate hitherto under the references to them, has given them the sanction of their approbation.

Considering therefore the law of proceedings in the Senate as composed of the precepts of the constitution, the regulations of the Senate, and where these are silent, of the rules of Parliament, I have here endeavored to collect and digest so much of these as is called for in ordinary practice, collating the Parliamentary with the Senatorial rules, both where they agree and where they vary. I have done this, as well to have them at hand for my own government, as to deposit with the Senate the standard by which I judge and am willing to be judged. I could not doubt the necessity of quoting the sources of my information; among which Mr. Hatsell's most valuable book is pre-eminent; but as he has only treated some general heads, I have been obliged to recur to other authorities in support of a number of common rules of practice to which his plan did not descend. Sometimes each authority cited supports the whole passage. Sometimes it rests on all taken together. Sometimes the authority goes only to a part of the text, the residue being inferred from known rules and principles. For some of the most familiar forms no written authority is or can be quoted; no writer having supposed it necessary to repeat what all were presumed to know. The statement of these must rest on their notoriety.

I am aware that authorities can often be produced in opposition to the rules which I lay down as parliamentary. An attention to dates will generally remove their weight. The proceedings of parliament in ancient times, and for a long while, were crude, multiform and embarrassing. They have been however constantly advancing towards uniformity and accuracy; and have now attained a degree of aptitude to their object, yond which little is to be desired or expected.

Yet I am far from the presumption of believing that I may not have mistaken the parliamentary practice in some cases; and especially in those minor forms, which, being practised daily, are supposed known to every body, and therefore have not been committed to writing. Our resources, in this quarter of the globe, for obtaining information on that part of the subject, are not perfect. But I have begun a sketch, which those who come after me will successively correct and fill up, till a code of rules shall be formed for the use of the Senate, the effects of which may be, accuracy in business, economy of time, order, uniformity, and impartiality.

NOTE.—The rules and practices peculiar to the SENATE are printed in *ITALICS*.

Those of PARLIAMENT are in the ROMAN LETTER.

IMPORTANCE OF RULES.

SEC. I.
THE IMPORTANCE OF ADHERING TO RULES.

MR. ONSLOW, the ablest among the Speakers of the House of Commons, used to say 'it was a maxim he had often heard when he was a young man, from old and experienced members, that nothing tended more to throw power into the hands of administration and those who acted with the majority of the House of Commons, than a neglect of, or departure from, the rules of proceeding: that these forms, as instituted by our ancestors, operated as a check and controul on the actions of the majority, and that they were in many instances, a shelter and protection to the minority, against the attempts of power.' So far the maxim is certainly true, and is founded in good sense, that as it is always in the power of the majority, by their numbers, to stop any improper measures proposed on the part of their opponents, the only weapons, by which the minority can defend themselves against similar attempts from those in power,

Importance of Rules

1

are the forms and rules of proceeding which have been adopted as they were found necessary from time to time, and are become the law of the house; by a strict adherence to which, the weaker party can only be protected from those irregularities and abuses which these forms were intended to check, and which the wantonness of power is but too often apt to suggest to large and successful majorities. 2 *Hats.* 171, 172.

And whether these forms be in all cases the most rational or not, is really not of so great importance. It is much more material that there should be a rule to go by, than what that rule is; that there may be an uniformity of proceeding in business, not subject to the caprice of the Speaker, or captiousness of the members. It is very material that order, decency and regularity be preserved in a dignified public body. 2 *Hats.* 149.

SEC. II.
LEGISLATURE.

Legislature

ALL Legislative powers, herein granted, shall be vested in a Congress of the United States, which shall consist of a Senate and House of Representatives. Constitution of the United States, Art. 1, Sec. 1.

The Senators and Representatives shall receive a compensation for their services, to be ascertained by law and paid out of the Treasury of the United States. Constitution of the United States, Art. 1. Sec. 6.

For the powers of Congress, see the following Articles and Sections of the Constitution of the United States. I. 4. 7. 8. 9. II. 1. 2. III. 3. IV. 1. 3. 5. *and all the amendments.*

SEC. III.
PRIVILEGE.

THE privileges of the members of parliament, from small and obscure beginnings, have been advancing for centuries, with a firm and never yielding pace. Claims seem to have been brought forward from time to time, and repeated, till some example of their admission enabled them to build law on that example. We can only therefore state the point of progression at which they now are. It is now acknowledged, 1st. That they are at all times exempted from question elsewhere for any thing said in their own house; that during the time of privilege, 2. Neither a member himself, his* wife, or his servants, [familiares sui]

Privilege

*Ord. of the H. of Com. 1663. July 16.

Privilege

for any matter of their own, may be* arrested, on mesne process, in any civil suit: 3. Nor be detained under execution, though levied before time of privilege: 4. Nor impleaded, cited, or subpoenaed in any court: 5. Nor summoned as a witness or juror: 6. Nor may their lands or goods be distrained: 7. Nor their persons assaulted, or characters traduced. And the period of time, covered by privilege, before and after the session, with the practice of short prorogations under the connivance of the crown, amounts in fact to a perpetual protection against the course of justice. In one instance indeed it has been relaxed by the 10. G. 3. c. 50, which permits judiciary proceedings to go on against them. That these privileges must be continually progressive seems to result from their rejecting all definition of them; the doctrine being that 'their dignity and independence are preserved by keeping their privileges indefinite;' and that 'the maxims upon which they proceed, together with the method of proceeding, rest entirely in their own breast, and are not defined and ascertained by any particular stated laws.' 1. *Blackst.* 163. 164.

It was probably from this view of the encroaching character of Privilege, that the framers

---

*Elsynge 217.1. Hats. 21.1. Grey's deb. 133.

of our constitution, in their care to provide that the laws shall bind equally on all, and especially that those who make them shall not exempt themselves from their operation, have only privileged 'Senators and Representatives' themselves from the single act of 'arrest in all cases, except treason, felony and breach of the peace, during their attendance at the session of their respective houses, and in going to and returning from the same, and from being questioned in any other place for any speech or debate in either house.' Const. U.S. Art. 1. Sec. 6. *Under the general authority 'to make all laws necessary and proper for carrying into execution the powers given them,'* Const. U.S. Art. 2. Sec. 8, *they may provide by law the details which may be necessary for giving full effect to the enjoyment of this privilege. No such law being as yet made, it seems to stand at present on the following ground. 1. The act of arrest is void ab initio.* 2. The member arrested may be discharged on motion. 1. Bl. 166. 2. Stra. 990, or by Habeas Corpus under the Federal or State authority, as the case may be; or by a writ of privilege out of the Chancery,* 2. Stra. 989, *in those states which have adopted that part of the laws of England.* Orders of the H. of Commons. 1550. February 20. 3. *The arrest being unlawful, is a trespass for which the officer and others concerned are liable to action*

**2. Stra. 989.

Protection
from Arrest

*or indictment in the ordinary courts of justice, as
in other cases of unauthorised arrest. 4. The court
before which the process is returnable, is bound to
act as in other cases of unauthorised proceeding,
and liable also, as in other similar cases, to have
their proceedings staid or corrected by the superior courts.*

*The time necessary for going to and re-
turning from Congress, not being defined, it will
of course be judged of in every particular case by
those who will have to decide the case.* While
privilege was understood in England to extend,
as it does here, only to exemption from arrest
eundo, morando, et redeundo, the House of
Commons themselves decided that 'a convenient time was to be understood.' (1580.) 1. *Hats.*
99, 100. Nor is the law so strict in point of time
as to require the party to set out immediately on his return, but allows him time to
settle his private affairs and to prepare for
his journey; and does not even scan his
road very nicely, nor forfeit his protection
for a little deviation from that which is
most direct; some necessity perhaps con-
straining him to it. 2. *Stra.* 986, 987.

This privilege from arrest, privileges
of course against all process the disobedience
to which is punishable by an attachment of
the person; as a subpoena ad respondendum,

or testificandum, or a summons on a jury: and with reason; because a member has superior duties to perform in another place. *When a representative is withdrawn from his seat by summons, the 30,000 people whom he represents lose their voice in debate and vote as they do on his voluntary absence: when a senator is withdrawn by summons his state loses half its voice in debate and vote, as it does on his voluntary absence. The enormous disparity of evil admits no comparison.*

So far there will probably be no difference of opinion as to the privileges of the two houses of congress: but in the following cases it is otherwise. In December 1795, the H. of R. committed two persons of the name of Randall and Whitney for attempting to corrupt the integrity of certain members, which they considered as a contempt and breach of the privileges of the house: and the facts being proved, Whitney was detained in confinement a fortnight, and Randall three weeks, and was reprimanded by the Speaker. —In March 1796, the H. of R. voted a challenge given to a member of their house to be a breach of the privileges of the house; but satisfactory apologies and acknowledgments being made, no further proceeding was had. —The editor of the Aurora having, in his paper of February 19, 1800, inserted some paragraphs defamatory of the Senate, and

Right to Legal Defense

failed in his appearance, he was ordered to be committed. In debating the legality of this order it was insisted, in support of it, that every man, by the law of nature, and every body of men, possesses the right of self defence; that all public functionaries are essentially invested with the powers of self-preservation; that they have an inherent right to do all acts necessary to keep themselves in a condition to discharge the trusts confided to them;

Law reigns supreme

that whenever authorities are given, the means of carrying them into execution are given by necessary implication; that thus we see the British parliament exercise the right of punishing contempts; all the state legislatures exercise the same power; and every court does the same; that if we have it not we sit at the mercy of every intruder who may enter our doors or gallery, and by noise, and tumult, render proceeding in business impracticable; that if our tranquillity is to be perpetually disturbed by newspaper defamation, it will not be possible to exercise our functions with the requisite coolness and deliberation; and that we must therefore have a power to punish these disturbers of our peace and proceedings. To this it was answered that the Parliament and courts of England have cognisance of contempts by the express provisions of their law; that the state legislatures have equal authority, because their powers are plenary; they represent their constituents completely, and possess all their powers, except such as their con-stitutions have expressly denied them; that the courts of the several states have the same powers by the laws of their states, and those of the federal government by the same state laws, adopted in each state by a law of Congress; that none of these bodies therefore derive those powers from natural or necessary right, but from express law; that Congress have no such natural or necessary power, nor any powers but such as are given them by the constitution; that that has given them directly ex-emption from personal arrest, exemption from question elsewhere for what is said in their house, and power over their own members and proceed-ings; for these no further law is necessary, the constitution being the law; that moreover, by that article of the constitution which authorises them 'to make all laws necessary and proper for carrying into execution the powers vested by the constitu-tion in them,' they may provide by law for an un-disturbed exercise of their functions, e.g. for the punishment of contempts, of affrays or tumult in their presence, &c; but, till the law be made, it does not exist; and does not exist, from their own ne-glect; that in the mean time, however, they are not unprotected, the ordinary magistrates and courts of law being open and competent to punish all unjustifiable disturbances or defamations, and even their own serjeant who may appoint depu-

Power of the Constitution

Checks and Balances

ties ad libitum to aid him, 3 Grey. 59. 147. 255,
is equal to small disturbances; that in requiring
a previous law, the constitution had regard to
the inviolability of the citizen as well as of the
member; as, should one house, in the regular
form of a bill, aim at too broad privileges, it may
be checked by the other, and both by the President; and also as, the law being promulgated,
the citizen will know how to avoid offence. But
if one branch may assume its own privileges
without controul, if it may do it on the spur of
the occasion, conceal the law in its own breast,
and, after the fact committed, make its sentence
both the law and the judgment on that fact; if
the offence is to be kept undefined, and to be
declared only ex re nata, and according to the
passions of the moment, and there be no limitation either in the manner or measure of the
punishment, the condition of the citizen will be
perilous indeed. —Which of these doctrines is to
prevail, time will decide. Where there is no fixed
law, the judgment on any particular case is the law
of that single case only, and dies with it. When a
new and even a similar case arises, the judgment
which is to make, and at the same time apply the
law, is open to question and consideration, as are
all new laws. —Perhaps Congress in the mean
time, in their care for the safety of the citizen, as
well as that for their own protection, may declare

by law what is necessary and proper to enable them to carry into execution the powers vested in them, and thereby hang up a rule for the inspection of all, which may direct the conduct of the citizen, and at the same time test the judgments they shall themselves pronounce in their own case.

House
Privileges

Privilege from arrest takes place by force of the election; and before a return be made, a member elected may be named of a committee, and is to every intent a member, except that he cannot vote until he is sworn. *Memor.* 107, 108. *D'Ewes* 642. *col.* 2, 643. *col.* 1. *Pet. miscel. parl.* 119. *Lex. Parl.* c. 23, 2. *Hats.* 22, 62.

Every man must, at his peril, take notice who are members of either house returned of record. *Lex. Parl.* 23, 4. *inst.* 24.

On complaint of a breach of privilege, the party may either be summoned, or sent for in custody of the serjeant. 1. *Grey*, 88, 95.

The privilege of a member is the privilege of the house. If the member waive it without leave, it is a ground for punishing him, but cannot in effect waive the privilege of the house. 3. *Grey*, 140, 222.

For any speech or debate in either house, they shall not be questioned in any other place. *Const. U. S.* I. 6. *S. P. Protest of the Commons to James I.* 1621. 2. *Rapin, No.* 54. pa. 211, 212. But this is restrained to things done in the

*The House
polices itself*

house in a parliamentary course. 1. *Rush.* 663. For he is not to have privilege contra morem parliamentarium; to exceed the bounds and limits of his place and duty. *Com. p.*

If an offence be committed by a member in the house, of which the house has cognisance, it is an infringement of their right for any person or court to take notice of it, till the house has punished the offender, or referred him to a due course. *Lex. Parl.* 63.

Privilege is in the power of the house, and is a restraint to the proceeding of inferior courts; but not of the house itself. 2. *Nalson* 450. 2. *Grey,* 399. For whatever is spoken in the house is subject to the censure of the house; and offences of this kind have been severely punished by calling the person to the bar to make submission, committing him to the tower, expelling the house, &c. *Scob.* 72. *L. Parl. c.* 22.

It is a breach of order for the Speaker to refuse to put a question which is in order. 2. *Hats.* 175. 6. 5. *Grey,* 133.

And even in cases of treason, felony, and breach of the peace, to which privilege does not extend as to substance, yet in parliament, a member is privileged as to the mode of proceeding. The case is first to be laid before the house, that it may judge of the fact and of the grounds of the accusation, and how far forth the manner of the trial may concern their privilege. Otherwise it would be in the power of other branches of the government, and even of every private man, under pretences of treason &c. to take any man from his service in the house, and so as many, one after another, as would make the house what he pleaseth. *Decl. of the Com. on the King's declaring Sir John Hotham a traitor. 4. Rushw.* 586. So when a member stood indicted of felony, it was adjudged that he ought to remain of the house till conviction. For it may be any man's case, who is guiltless, to be accused and indicted of felony, or the like crime. 23. *El.* 1580. *D'Ewes.* 283. *col.* 1. *Lex. Parl.* 133.

Trial by the members themselves

    When it is found necessary for the public service to put a member under arrest, or when, on any public enquiry, matter comes out which may lead to affect the person of a member, it is the practice immediately to acquaint the house, that they may know the reasons for such a proceeding, and take such steps as they think proper. 2. *Hats.* 259. Of which see many examples. *Ib.* 256. 257. 258. But the communication is subsequent to the arrest. 1. *Blackst.* 167.

In case of arrest

    It is highly expedient, says Hatsell, for the due preservation of the privileges of the separate branches of the legislature,

Equal but separate branches

that neither should encroach on the other, or interfere in any matter depending before them, so as to preclude, or even influence that freedom of debate, which is essential to a free council. They are therefore not to take notice of any bills or other matters depending, or of votes that have been given, or of speeches which have been held, by the members of either of the other branches of the legislature, until the same have been communicated to them in the usual parliamentary manner. 2. *Hats.* 252. 4. *Inst.* 15. *Seld. Jud.* 53. Thus the king's taking notice of the bill for suppressing soldiers, depending before the house, his proposing a provisional clause for a bill before it was presented to him by the two houses; his expressing displeasure against some persons for matters moved in parliament during the debate and preparation of a bill, were breaches of privilege. 2. *Nalson*, 743. and in 1783, December 17, it was declared a breach of fundamental privileges, &c. to report any opinion or pretended opinion of the king on any bill or proceeding depending in either house of parliament, with a view to influence the votes of the members. 2. *Hats.* 251, 6.

SEC. IV.
ELECTIONS.

THE *times, places, and manner of holding Elections for Senators and Representatives, shall be prescribed in each state by the legislature thereof; but the Congress may, at any time, by law, make or alter such regulations, except as to the places of chusing Senators.* Constitution I. 4.

States regulate elections

      Each house shall be the judge of the elections, returns, and qualifications of its own members. Constitution I. 5.

SEC. V.
QUALIFICATIONS.

THE *Senate of the United States shall be composed of two Senators from each state, chosen by the legislature thereof for six years, and each Senator shall have one vote.*

Senators

      Immediately after they shall be assembled in consequence of the first election, they shall be divided as equally as may be into three classes. The seats of the Senators of the 1st class shall be vacated at the end of the 2d year; of the second class at the expiration of the 4th year; and of the 3d class at the expiration of the 6th year; so that one third may be chosen every second year; and if vacancies happen by resignation or otherwise, during the recess of the legislature of any state, the Executive thereof may make temporary appointments, until the next meeting of the legislature which shall then fill such vacancies.

No person shall be a Senator who shall not have attained to the age of 30 years, and been 9 years a citizen of the United States, and who shall not, when elected, be an inhabitant of that state for which he shall be chosen. Constitution I. 3.

Representatives

The House of Representatives shall be composed of members chosen every second year by the people of the several states; and the electors in each state shall have the qualifications requisite for electors of the most numerous branch of the state legislature.

No person shall be a Representative who shall not have attained to the age of 25 years, and been 7 years a citizen of the United States, and who shall not, when elected, be an inhabitant of that state in which he shall be chosen.

Representatives and direct taxes shall be apportioned among the several states which may be included within this Union, according to their respective numbers, which shall be determined by adding to the whole number of free persons, including those bound to service for a term of years, and including Indians not taxed, three fifths of all other persons. The actual enumeration shall be made within three years after the first meeting of the Congress of the United States, and within every subsequent term of ten years, in such manner as they shall be law direct. The number of representatives shall not exceed one for every thirty thousand, but each state shall have at least one representative. Constitution of the United States I. 2.

The provisional apportionments of Representatives made in the constitution in 1787, and afterwards by Congress, were as follows:

Provisional apportionments

	1787	1793	1801
New Hampshire	3	4	
Massachusetts	8	14	
Rhode Island	1	2	
Counecticut	5	7	
Vermont		2	
New-York	6	10	
Jersey	4	5	
Pennsylvania	8	13	
Delaware	1	1	
Maryland	6	8	
Virginia	10	19	
Kentucky		2	
Tennessee			
N.Carolina	5	10	
S. Carolina	5	6	
Georgia	3	2	

When vacancies happen in the Representation from any state, the Executive authority thereof shall issue writs of election to fill such vacancies. Constitution I. 2.

Restrictions

No Senator or Representative shall, during the time for which he was elected, be appointed to any civil office under the authority of the United States which shall have been created, or the emoluments whereof shall have been increased, during such time; and no person holding any office under the United States, shall be a member of either house during his continuance in office. Constitution I. 6.

SEC. VI.
QUORUM.

A quorum is necessary to do business

A MAJORITY of each house shall constitute a Quorum to do business: but a smaller number may adjourn from day to day, and may be authorised to compel the attendance of absent members, in such manner, and under such penalties as each house may provide. Constitution I. 5.

In general the chair is not to be taken till a Quorum for business is present; unless, after due waiting, such a quorum be despaired of; when the chair may be taken and the house adjourned. And whenever, during business, it is observed that a Quorum is not present, any member may call for the house to be counted, and being found deficient, business is suspended. 2. *Hats*. 125. 126.

The President having taken the chair, and a Quorum being present, the journal of the preceding day shall be read, to the end that any mistake may be corrected that shall have been made in the entries. Rules of Senate, 1.

SEC. VII.
CALL OF THE HOUSE.

ON a call of the house, each person rises up as he is called, and answereth. The absentees are then only noted, but no excuse to be made till the house be fully called over. Then the absentees are called a second time, and if still absent, excuses are to be heard. *Ord. H. Com.* 92.

Roll call

They rise that their persons may be recognized; the voice, in such a crowd, being an insufficient verification of their presence. But in so small a body as the Senate of the United States, the trouble of rising cannot be necessary.

Orders for calls on different days may subsist at the same time. 2 *Hats*. 72.

SEC. VIII.
ABSENCE.

No absence without leave

NO member shall absent himself from the service of the Senate, without leave of the Senate first obtained. And in case a less number than a Quorum of the Senate shall convene, they are hereby authorised to send the Serjeant at arms, or any other person or persons by them authorised, for any or all absent members, as the majority of such members present shall agree, at the expense of such absent members respectively, unless such excuse for non-attendance shall be made, as the Senate, when a Quorum is convened, shall judge sufficient: and in that case, the expense shall be paid out of the contingent fund. And this rule shall apply as well to the first convention of Senate, at the legal time of meeting, as to each day of the session, after the hour is arrived to which the Senate stood adjourned. Rule 19.

SEC. IX.
SPEAKER.

Role of the Vice President

THE Vice-President of the United States shall be President of the Senate, but shall have no vote unless they be equally divided. Constitution I. 3.

The Senate shall chuse their other officers and also a President pro tempore in the absence of the Vice President, or when he shall exercise the office of President of the United States. ib.

The House of Representatives shall chuse their Speaker and other officers. Constitution I. 2.

Speaker of the House

When but one person is proposed, and no objection made, it has not been usual in parliament to put any question to the House; but without a question, the members proposing him conduct him to the chair. But if there be objection, or another proposed, a question is put by the clerk. 2. *Hats.* 158. As are also questions of adjournment. 6. *Grey,* 406. Where the house debated and exchanged messages and answers with the king for a week, without a Speaker, till they were prorogued. They have done it de diem in diem for 14 days, 1. *Chand.* 331. 335.

In the Senate, a President pro tempore in the absence of the Vice President is proposed and chosen by ballot. His office is understood to be determined on the Vice President's appearing and taking the chair, or at the meeting of the Senate after the first recess.

Temporary appointments

Where the Speaker has been ill,

Pro tem
appointees

other Speakers pro tempore have been appointed. Instances of this are 1. *H.* 4. Sir John Cheyney, and so Sir William Sturton, and in 15. *H.* 6. Sir John Tyrrel, in 1656, January 27. 1658, March 9. 1659, January 13.

　　Sir Job. Charlton ill.
Seymour chosen,
1673, February 18.
　　Seymour being ill,
Sir Robt. Sawyer chosen,
1678, April 15.
　　Sawyer being ill,
Seymour chosen.

Not merely pro tem.
1 *Chand.* 169. 276, 277.

Thorpe in execution, a new Speaker chosen, 31 *H. VI.* 3 *Grey*, 11. and March 14, 1694, Sir John Trevor chosen. There have been no later instances 2 *Hats.* 161. 4 *Inst.* 8 *L. Parl.* 263.

　　A Speaker may be removed at the will of the house and a Speaker pro tempore appointed. 2 *Grey*, 186. 5 *Grey*, 134.

SEC. X.
ADDRESS.

State of the
Union
address

THE President shall from time to time give to the Congress information of the state of the Union, and recommend to their consideration such measures as he shall judge necessary and expedient. Constitution II. 3.

A joint address of both houses of parliament is read by the Speaker of the House of Lords. It may be attended by both houses in a body, or by a Committee from each house, or by the two Speakers only. An Address of the House of Commons only, may be presented by the whole house, or by the Speaker, 9 *Grey* 473. 1 *Chandler*, 298, 301, or by such particular members as are of the Privy council. 2 *Hats.* 278.

SEC. XI.
COMMITTEES.

STANDING committees, as of Privileges and Elections, &c. are usually appointed at the first meeting, to continue through the session. The person first named is generally permitted to act as chairman. But this is a matter of courtesy; every committee having a right to elect their own chairman, who presides over them, puts questions, and reports their proceedings to the House. 4 inst. 11. 12. *Scob.* 9. 1. *Grey*, 122.

Standing Committees

At these committees the members are to speak standing and not sitting: though there is reason to conjecture it was formerly otherwise. *D'Ewes,* 630. *col.* I. 4. *Parl. hist.* 440. 2 *Hats.* 77.

Hearings are not public

Their proceedings are not to be published, as they are of no force till confirmed by the house. *Rushw. part.* 3. *vol.* 2. 74. 3. *Grey* 401. *Scob.* 39. Nor can they receive a petition but through the house. 9. *Grey* 412.

When a committee is charged with an enquiry, if a member prove to be involved, they cannot proceed against him, but must make a special report to the House, whereupon the member is heard in his place, or at the bar, or a special authority is given to the committee to enquire concerning him. 9. *Grey,* 523.

So soon as the house sits, and a committee is notified of it, the chairman is in duty bound to rise instantly, and the members to attend the service of the house. 2. *Nals.* 319.

It appears that on joint committees of the Lords and Commons, each committee acted integrally in the following instances. 7 *Grey,* 261, 278, 285, 338. 1 *Chandler,* 357, 462. In the following instances it does not appear whether they did or not. 6 *Grey,* 129. 7 *Grey,* 213, 229, 321.

SEC. XII.
COMMITTEE OF THE WHOLE.

THE speech, messages and other matters of great concernment, are usually referred to a committee of the whole house. 6 *Grey*, 311. Where general principles are digested in the form of resolutions, which are debated and amended till they get into a shape which meets the approbation of a majority. These being reported and confirmed by the house, are then referred to one or more select committees, according as the subject divides itself into one or more bills. *Scob.* 36. 44. Propositions for any charge on the people are especially to be first made in a committee of the whole. 3 *Hats.* 127. The sense of the whole is better taken in committee, because in all committees every one speaks as often as he pleases. *Scob.* 49. They generally acquiesce in the chairman named by the Speaker: but, as well as all other committees, have a right to elect one, some member, by consent, putting the question. *Scob.* 36. 3 *Grey*, 301. The form of going from the house into committee, is for the Speaker, on motion, to put the question that the house do now resolve itself into a committee of the whole to take under consideration such a matter, naming it. If determined in the affirmative, he leaves the chair, and takes a seat elsewhere, as any other member; and the person appointed chairman seats himself at the clerk's table. *Scob.* 36. Their Quorum is the same as that of the house; and if a defect happens, the Chairman, on a motion

All members discuss important matters

Committee of the whole

and question, rises, the Speaker resumes the chair, and the chairman can make no other report than to inform the house of the cause of their dissolution. If a message is announced during a committee, the Speaker takes the chair, and receives it, because the committee cannot. 2. *Hats*. 125. 126.

In a committee of the whole, the tellers on a division, differing as to the numbers, great heats and confusion arose, and danger of a decision by the sword. The Speaker took the chair, the mace was forcibly laid on the table, whereupon, the members retiring to their places, the Speaker told the house 'he had taken the chair without an order, to bring the house into order.' Some excepted against it; but it was generally approved as the only expedient to suppress the disorder. And every member was required, standing up in his place, to engage that he would proceed no further in consequence of what had happened in the grand committee, which was done. 3 *Grey*, 128.

A committee of the whole being broken up in disorder, and the chair resumed by the Speaker without an order, the house was adjourned. The next day the committee was considered as thereby dissolved, and the subject again before the house; and it was decided in the house, without returning into committee. 3 *Grey*, 130.

No Previous question can be put in a committee; nor can this committee adjourn as others may; but if their business is unfinished, they rise, on a question, the house is resumed, and the chairman reports that the committee of the whole have, according to order, had under their consideration such a matter and have made progress therein; but not having had time to go through the same, have directed him to ask leave to sit again. Whereupon a question is put on their having leave, and on the time when the house will again resolve itself into a committee. *Scob.* 38. But if they have gone through the matter referred to them, a member moves that the committee may rise, and the chairman report their proceedings to the house; which being resolved, the chairman rises, the Speaker resumes the chair, the chairman informs him that the committee have gone through the business referred to them, and that he is ready to make report when the house shall think proper to receive it. If the house have time to receive it, there is usually a cry of 'now, now,' whereupon he makes the report: but if it be late, the cry is 'to-morrow, to-morrow,' or 'on Monday, &c.' or a motion is made to that effect, and

Old business, New business

a question put that it be received, to-morrow, &c. *Scob.* 38.

In other things the rules of proceeding are to be the same as in the House. *Scob.* 39.

SEC. XIII.
EXAMINATION OF WITNESSES.

COMMON fame is a good ground for the house to proceed by enquiry, and even to accusation. *Resolution House Commons* 1. *Car.* 1. 1625. *Rush. L. Parl.* 115. 1. *Grey.* 16—22. 92. 8 *Grey.* 21, 23, 27, 45.

Witnesses are not to be produced but where the house has previously instituted an enquiry, 2 *Hats.* 102. nor then are orders for their attendance given blank, 3 *Grey.* 51.

Role of the Speaker

When any person is examined before a committee, or at the bar of the house, any member wishing to ask the person a question, must address it to the Speaker or Chairman, who repeats the question to the person, or says to him, 'you hear the question, answer it.' But if the propriety of the question be objected to, the Speaker directs the witness, counsel and parties, to withdraw; for no question can be moved or put, or debated while they are there. 2. *Hats.* 108. Sometimes the questions are previously settled in writing before the witness enters. *ib.* 106, 107. 8. *Grey* 64. The questions asked must be entered in the Journals. 3. *Grey* 81. But the testimony given in answer before the house is never written down; but before a committee it must be, for the information of the house who are not present to hear it. 7. *Grey* 52. 334.

If either house have occasion for the presence of a person in custody of the other, they ask the other their leave that he may be brought up to them in custody. 3. *Hats.* 52.

A member, in his place, gives information to the house of what he knows of any matter under hearing at the bar. *Jour. H. of C. Jan.* 22, 1744—5.

Either house may request, but not command the attendance of a member of the other. They are to make the request by message to the other house, and to express clearly the purpose of attendance, that no improper subject of examination may be tendered to him. The house then gives leave to the member to attend, if he chuse it; waiting first to know from the member himself whether he chuses to attend, till which they do not take the message into consideration. But when the peers are sitting as a court of criminal judicature, they

Requesting the presence of a member from another branch

may order attendance; unless where it be
a case of impeachment by the Commons.
There it is to be a request. 3 *Hats.* 17. 9.
Grey. 306. 406. 10. *Grey.* 133.

Counsel are to be heard only on
private, not on public bills, and on such
points of law only as the house shall direct.
10. *Grey.* 61.

SEC. XIV.
ARRANGEMENT OF BUSINESS.

Speaker arranges order of business

THE Speaker is not precisely bound to any
rules as to what bills or other matter shall be
first taken up, but is left to his own discretion,
unless the house on a question decide to take
up a particular subject. *Hakew.* 136.

A settled order of business is, however,
necessary for the government of the presiding
person, and to restrain individual members from
calling up favorite measures, or matters under
their special patronage, out of their just turn. It
is useful also for directing the discretion of the
house, when they are moved to take up a particular matter, to the prejudice of others having
priority of right to their attention in the general
order of business.

*In Senate, the bills and other papers which
are in possession of the house, and in a state to be acted*

on, are arranged every morning, and brought on in
the following order.

    1. Bills ready for a 2nd reading are read,
that they may be referred to committees, and so
be put under way. But if, on their being read, no
motion is made for commitment, they are then laid
on the table in the general file, to be taken up in
their just turn.

    2. After XII. o'clock, bills ready for it are
put on their passage.

    3. Reports in possession of the House,
which offer grounds for a bill, are to be taken up,
that the bill may be ordered in.

    4. Bills or other matters before the house and
unfinished on the preceding day, whether taken up
in turn, or on special order, are entitled to be resumed
and passed on through their present stage.

    5. These matters being dispatched, for
preparing and expediting business, the general
file of bills and other papers is then taken up,
and each article of it is brought on according
to its seniority, reckoned by the date of its first
introduction to the house. Reports on bills be-
long to the dates of their bills.

    In this way we do not waste our time in
debating what shall be taken up: we do one thing
at a time; follow up a subject while it is fresh, and
till it is done with; clear the house of business
gradatim as it is brought on, and prevent, to a

Order of business

One thing at a time

certain degree, its immense accumulation towards the close of the session.

Communication between the houses

Arrangement however can only take hold of matters in possession of the house. New matter may be moved at any time, when no question is before the house. Such are original motions, and reports on bills. Such are bills from the other house, which are received at all times, and receive their first reading as soon as the question then before the house is disposed of; and Bills brought in on leave, which are read first whenever presented. So messages from the other house respecting amendments to bills are taken up as soon as the house is clear of a question, unless they require to be printed, for better consideration. Orders of the day may be called for, even when another question is before the house.

SEC. XV.
ORDER.

Responsibility for order

EACH house may determine the rules of its proceedings; punish its members for disorderly behaviour, and with the concurrence of two thirds expel a member. Constitution I. 5.

In parliament 'instances make order' per Speaker Onslow. 2 *Hats.* 141. but what is done only by one parliament, cannot be called Custom of parliament by Prynne. 1 *Grey* 52.

SEC. XVI.
ORDER RESPECTING PAPERS.

THE clerk is to let no journals, records, accounts, or papers be taken from the table, or out of his custody. 2. *Hats.* 193. 194.

Role of the Clerk

    Mr. Prynne having at a committee of the whole amended a mistake in a bill without order or knowledge of the committee was reprimanded. 1 *Chand.* 77.

    A bill being missing, the house resolved that a protestation should be made and subscribed by the members 'before Almighty God and this honourable house that neither myself nor any other to my knowledge, have taken away, or do at this present conceal a bill entitled, &c.' 5 *Grey.* 202.

    After a Bill is engrossed, it is put into the Speaker's hands, and he is not to let anyone have it to look into. *Town. col.* 209.

SEC. XVII.
ORDER IN DEBATE.

WHEN the Speaker is seated in his chair, every member is to sit in his place. *Scob.* 6. 3, *Grey,* 403.

    When any member means to speak, he is to stand up in his place, uncovered, and to

Speaker maintains order in debate

address himself, not to the House, or any particular member, but to the Speaker, who calls him by his name, that the house may take notice who it is that speaks. *Scob.* 6. *D'Ewes* 487. *Col.* 1. 2 *Hats.* 77. 4 *Grey* 66. 8 *Grey* 108. But members who are indisposed may be indulged to speak sitting. 2 *Hats.* 75. 77. 1. *Grey* 195.

In Senate every member, when he speaks, shall address the chair standing in his place, and when he has finished shall sit down. Rule 3.

When a member stands up to speak, no question is to be put, but he is to be heard, unless the House overrule him. 4 *Grey* 390. 5 *Grey* 6. 143.

If two or more rise to speak nearly together, the Speaker determines who was first up, and calls him by name, whereupon he proceeds, unless he voluntarily sits down and gives way to the other. But sometimes the house does not acquiesce in the Speaker's decision, in which case the question is put 'which member was first up?' 2 *Hats.* 76. *Scob.* 7. *D'Ewes* 434. col. 1, 2.

In the Senate of the United States, the President's decision is without appeal. Their rule is in these words: When two members rise at the same time, the President shall name the person to speak; but in all cases, the member first rising, shall speak first. Rule 5.

A Manual of Parliamentary Practice

Limiting speech on a subject

No man may speak more than once to the same bill on the same day; or even on another day if the debate be adjourned. But if it be read more than once in the same day, he may speak once at every reading. *Co.* 12. 116. *Hakew.* 148. *Scob.* 58. 2 *Hats.* 75. Even a change of opinion does not give a right to be heard a second time. *Smyth Comw. L.* 2. *c.* 3. *Arcan. Parl.* 17.

The corresponding rule of Senate is in these words: No member shall speak more than twice in any one debate on the same day, without leave of the Senate. Rule 4.

But he may be permitted to speak again to clear a matter of fact. 3. *Grey* 357. 416. Or merely to explain himself. 2. *Hats.* 73. in some material part of his speech. *ib.* 75. or to the manner or words of the question, keeping himself to that only and not travelling into the merits of it. *Memorials* in *Hakew.* 29. or to the orders of the House if they be transgressed, keeping within that line, and not falling into the matter itself. *Mem.* in *Hakew.* 30, 31.

But if the Speaker rises to speak, the member standing up ought to sit down, that he may be first heard. *Town col.* 205. *Hale parl.* 133. *Mem.* in *Hakew.* 30. 31. Nevertheless, though the Speaker may of right speak to matters of order and be first heard, he is restrained from speaking on any other subject, except where the house have occasion for facts within his knowledge; then he may, with their leave, state the matter of fact. 3. *Grey* 38.

Some rules governing speeches

No one is to speak impertinently or beside the question, superfluously or tediously. *Scob.* 31. 33. 2. *Hats.* 166. 168. *Hale parl.* 133.

No person is to use indecent language against the proceedings of the house, no prior determination of which is to be reflected on by any member, unless he means to conclude with a motion to rescind it. 2 *Hats.* 169. 170. *Rushw. p.* 3. *v.* 1. *fol.* 42. But while a proposition is under consideration, is still in fieri, though it has even been reported by a committee, reflections on it are no reflections on the house. 9 *Grey,* 508.

No person in speaking, is to mention a member then present by his name; but to describe him by his seat in the house, or who spoke last, or on the other side of the question, &c. *Mem.* in *Hakew.* 3. *Smyth's Comw. L.* 2. *c.* 3. nor to digress from the matter to fall upon the person, *Scob.* 31. *Hale parl.* 133. 2. *Hats.* 166. by speaking, reviling, nipping, or unmannerly words against a particular member. *Smyth's Comw. L.* 2. *c.* 3. The consequences of a measure may be reprobated in strong terms; but to arraign the motives of those who propose or advocate it, is a personality, and against order. *Qui digreditur a materia ad personam,* Mr. Speaker ought to suppress. *Ord. Com.* 1604. *Apr.* 19.

When a member shall be called to order, he shall sit down until the President shall have determined whether he is in order or not. *Rule* 16.

No member shall speak to another, or otherwise interrupt the business of the Senate, or read any printed paper while the Journals or public papers are reading, or when any member is speaking in any debate. Rule 2.

No one is to disturb another in his speech by hissing, coughing, spitting, 6 *Grey,* 332. *Scob.* 8. *D'Ewes* 332. *col.* I. 640. *col.* 2. speaking or whispering to another. *Scob.* 6. *D'Ewes* 487. *col.* I. nor to stand up or interrupt him. *Town. col.* 205. *Mem.* in *Hakew.* 31. nor to pass between the Speaker and the speaking member, nor to go across the house. *Scob.* 6. or to walk up and down it, or to take books or papers from the table, or write there. 2. *Hats.* 171.

Nevertheless, if a member finds that it is not the inclination of the House to hear him, and that by conversation or any other noise they endeavour to drown his voice, it is his most prudent way to submit to the pleasure of the House, and sit down; for it scarcely ever happens that they are guilty of this piece of ill manners without sufficient reason, or inattentive to a member who says any thing worth their hearing. 2. *Hats.* 77. 78.

Punitive measures   If repeated calls do not produce order, the Speaker may call by his name any member obstinately persisting in irregularity, whereupon the house may require the member to withdraw. He is then to be heard in exculpation, and to withdraw. Then the Speaker states the offence committed, and the house considers the degree of punishment they will inflict. 2 *Hats.* 167. 7. 8. 172.

For instances of assaults and affrays in the House of Commons, and the proceedings thereon, see 1. *Pet. Misc.* 82. 3 *Grey,* 128. 4 *Grey,* 328. 5 *Grey,* 382. 6 *Grey,* 254. 10. *Grey,* 8. Whenever warm words, or an assault, have passed between members, the house, for the protection of their members, requires them to declare in their places not to prosecute any quarrel, 3 *Grey,*128. 293. 5 *Grey,* 289. or orders them to attend the Speaker, who is to accommodate their differences and report to the house. 3 *Grey,* 419. and they are put under restraint if they refuse, or until they do. 9 *Grey,* 234. 312.

Disorderly words are not to be noticed till the member has finished his speech.

5 *Grey*, 356. 6 *Grey*, 60. Then the person objecting to them, and desiring them to be taken down by the clerk at the table, must repeat them. The Speaker then may direct the clerk to take them down in his minutes. But if he thinks them not disorderly, he delays the direction. If the call becomes pretty general, he orders the clerk to take them down, as stated by the objecting member. They are then part of his minutes, and when read to the offending member, he may deny they were his words, and the house must then decide by a question whether they are his words or not. Then the member may justify them, or explain the sense in which he used them, or apologize. If the house is satisfied, no farther proceeding is necessary. But if two members still insist to take the sense of the house, the member must withdraw, before that question is stated, and then the sense of the house is to be taken. 2 *Hats*. 199. 4 *Grey*, 170. 6 *Grey*, 59. When any member has spoken, or other business intervened, after offensive words spoken, they cannot be taken notice of for censure. And this is for the common security of all, and to prevent mistakes which must happen if words are not taken down immediately. Formerly

Disorderly words

they might be taken down any time the same day. 2 *Hats.* 196. *Mem.* in *Hakew.* 71. 3 *Grey*, 48. 9 *Grey*, 514.

Disorderly words spoken in a committee must be written down as in the house; but the committee can only report them to the house for animadversion. 6 *Grey*, 46.

The rule of the Senate says if a member be called to order for words spoken, the exceptionable words shall be immediately taken down in writing, that the President may be better enabled to judge. Rule 17.

In parliament to speak irreverently or seditiously against the king is against order, *Smyth's Comw. L.* 2. *c.* 3. 2 *Hats.* 170.

Each house debates its own issues

It is a breach of order in debate to notice what has been said on the same subject in the other house, or the particular votes or majorities on it there: because the opinion of each house should be left to its own independency, not to be influenced by the proceedings of the other; and the quoting them might beget reflections leading to a misunderstanding between the two houses. 8 *Grey*, 22.

Neither house can exercise any authority over a member or officer of the other, but should complain to the house of which he is, and leave the punishment to them. Where the complaint is of words disrespectfully spoken by a member of another house, it is difficult to obtain punishment, because of the rules supposed necessary to be observed (as to the immediate noting down of words) for the security of members. Therefore it is the duty of the House and more particularly of the Speaker to interfere immediately, and not to permit expressions to go unnoticed which may give a ground of complaint to the other House, and introduce proceedings and mutual accusations between the two houses, which can hardly be terminated without difficulty and disorder. 3 *Hats.* 51.

Each house disciplines its own members

No member may be present when a bill or any business concerning himself is debating; nor is any member to speak to the merits of it till he withdraws. 2 *Hats.* 219. The rule is that if a charge against a member arise out of a report of a committee, or examination of witnesses in the house, as the member knows from that to what points he is to direct his exculpation, he may be heard to those points, before any question is moved or stated against him. He is then to be heard, and withdraw before any question is moved. But if the question itself is the charge, as for

*When
members
must absent
themselves*

breach of order, or matter arising in the debate, there the charge must be stated, that is, the question must be moved, himself heard, and then to withdraw. 2 *Hats.* 121. 122.

Where the private interests of a member are concerned in a bill or question, he is to withdraw. And where such an interest has appeared, his voice has been disallowed, even after a division. In a case so contrary not only to the laws of decency, but to the fundamental principle of the social compact, which denies to any man to be a judge in his own cause, it is for the honor of the house that this rule, of immemorial observance, should be strictly adhered to. 2 *Hats.* 119. 121. 6 *Grey,* 368.

No member is to come into the house with his head covered, nor to remove from one place to another with his hat on, nor is to put on his hat in coming in, or removing until he be set down in his place. *Scob.* 6.

A question of order may be adjourned to give time to look into precedents. 2 *Hats.* 118.

In the Senate of the United States, every question of order is to be decided by the President, without debate: but if there be a doubt in his mind, he may call for the sense of the Senate. Rule 16.

In parliament, all decisions of the Speaker may be controuled by the house. 3 *Grey,* 319.

SEC. XVIII.
ORDERS OF THE HOUSE.

OF right, the door of the house ought not to be shut, but to be kept by porters, or serjeants at arms, assigned for that purpose. *Mod. ten. Parl.* 23.

Behind closed doors

By the rules of the Senate, on motion made and seconded, to shut the doors of the Senate on the discussion of any business, which may in the opinion of a member require secrecy, the President shall direct the gallery to be cleared, and during the discussion of such motion, the doors shall remain shut. Rule 28.

No motion shall be deemed in order to admit any person or persons whatever within the doors of the Senate Chamber, to present any petition, memorial, or address, or to hear any such read. Rule 29.

The only case where a member has a right to insist on any thing is where he calls for the execution of a subsisting order of the house. Here, there having been already a resolution, any member had a right to insist that the Speaker, or any other whose duty it is, shall carry it into execution; and no debate or delay can be had on it. Thus any member has a right to have the house or gallery cleared of strangers, an order existing for that purpose; or to have the house told when there is not a quorum present. 2 *Hats.* 87. 129. How far an order of the house is binding, see *Hakew.* 392.

Orders of the day

But where an order is made that any particular matter be taken up on a particular day, there a question is to be put when it is called for, whether the house will now proceed to that matter? Where orders of the day are on important or interesting matter, they ought not to be proceeded on till an hour at which the house is usually full (*which in Senate is at noon.*)

Orders of the day may be discharged at any time, and a new one made for a different day. 3 *Grey,* 48. 313.

When a session is drawing to a close, and the important bills are all brought in, the house, in order to prevent interruption by further unimportant bills, sometimes come to a resolution that no new bill be brought in, except it be sent from the other house. 3 *Grey,* 156.

All orders of the house determine with the session; and one taken under such an order may, after the session is ended, be discharged on a habeas corpus. *Raym.* 120. *Jacob's L. D. by Ruffhead. Parliament,* 1 *Lev.* 165. *Prichard's case.*

*Where the Constitution authorises each
house to determine the Rules of its proceedings,
it must mean in those cases legislative, executive or judiciary, submitted to them by the
constitution, or in something relating to these,
and necessary towards their execution. But orders and resolutions are sometimes entered in
the journals, having no relation to these, such
as acceptances of invitations to attend orations,
to take part in processions, &c. These must be
understood to be merely conventional among
those who are willing to participate in the ceremony, and are therefore, perhaps, improperly
placed among the records of the house.*

SEC. XIX.
PETITIONS.

A PETITION prays something. A remonstrance
has no prayer. 1. *Grey*, 58.

Petitions must be subscribed by the
petitioners. *Scob.* 87. *L. Parl. c.* 22. 9. *Grey*
362. unless they are attending, 1. *Grey* 401.
or unable to sign, and averred by a member. 3 *Grey*, 418. But a petition not subscribed, but which the member presenting
it affirmed to be all in the hand writing of
the petitioner, and his name written in the

Petitions

beginning, was on the question (Mar. 14. 1800) received by the Senate. The averment of a member or of somebody without doors that they know the hand writing of the petitioners is necessary if it be questioned. 6. *Grey*, 36. It must be presented by a member, not by the petitioners, and must be opened by him, holding it in his hand. 10. *Grey*, 57.

Before any petition or memorial addressed to the Senate shall be received and read at the table, whether the same shall be introduced by the President or a member, a brief statement of the contents of the petition or memorial shall verbally be made by the introducer. Rule 21.

Regularly a motion for receiving it must be made and seconded, and a question put whether it shall be received? But a cry from the house of 'received,' or even its silence, dispenses with the formality of this question. It is then to be read at the table and disposed of.

SEC. XX.
MOTIONS.

Motions must be seconded

WHEN a motion has been made, it is not to be put to the question or debated until it is seconded. *Scob.* 21.

The Senate say no motion shall be debated until the same shall be seconded. *Rule* 6.

It is then and not till then in possession of the house, and cannot be withdrawn but by leave of the house. It is to be put into writing, if the House or Speaker require it, and must be read to the House by the Speaker as often as any member desires it for his information. 2. *Hats.* 82.

The rule of the Senate is when a motion shall be made and seconded, it shall be reduced to writing, if desired by the President, or any member, delivered in at the table, and read by the President before the same shall be debated. *Rule* 7.

It might be asked whether a motion for adjournment or for the orders of the day can be made by one member while another is speaking? It cannot. When two members offer to speak, he who rose first is to be heard, and it is a breach of order in another, to interrupt him, unless by calling him to order, if he departs from it. And the Question of order being decided, he is still to be heard through. A call for adjournment, or for the order of the day, or for the question, by gentlemen from their seats, is not a motion. No motion can be made without rising and

Questions of order

addressing the chair. Such calls are themselves breaches of order, which though the member who has risen may respect, as an expression of the impatience of the house against further debate, yet, if he chuses, he has a right to go on.

SEC. XXI.
RESOLUTIONS.

Resolutions are not binding

WHEN the House commands, it is by an 'order.' But facts, principles, their own opinions, and purposes, are expressed in the form of Resolutions.

A Resolution, for an allowance of money to the clerks, being moved, it was objected to as not in order, and so ruled by the chair. But on an appeal to the Senate [i.e. a call for their sense by the President on account of doubt in his mind according to Rule 16.] the decision was overruled. Journ. Sen. June 1, 1796. *I presume the doubt was, whether an allowance of money could be made otherwise than by bill.*

SEC. XXII.
BILLS.

Three readings

EVERY bill shall receive three readings, previous to its being passed; and the President shall give notice at each whether it be the 1st, 2nd, or 3d; which readings shall be on three different days, unless the Senate unanimously direct otherwise. *Rule* 13.

SEC. XXIII.
BILLS, LEAVE TO BRING IN.

ONE day's notice at least shall be given of an intended motion for leave to bring in a bill. Rule 12.

Requirements

When a member desires to bring in a bill on any subject, he states to the house in general terms the causes for doing it, and concludes by moving for leave to bring in a bill intituled, &c. Leave being given, on the question, a committee is appointed to prepare and bring in the bill. The mover and seconder are always appointed of this committee, and one or more in addition. *Hakew.* 132. *Scob.* 40.

It is to be presented fairly written, without any erasure or interlineation, or the Speaker may refuse it. *Scob.* 41. 1 *Grey,* 82. 84.

SEC. XXIV.
BILLS, FIRST READING.

WHEN a bill is first presented, the clerk reads it at the table, and hands it to the Speaker, who, rising, states to the house the title of the

No
amendment
at 1st reading

bill, that this is the 1st time of reading it, and the question will be whether it shall be read a 2nd time? Then sitting down to give an opening for objections, if none be made, he rises again and puts the question whether it shall be read a 2nd time? *Hakew*. 137. 141. A bill cannot be amended at the first reading. 6 *Grey*, 286. nor is it usual for it to be opposed then: but it may be done and rejected. *D'Ewes*, 335, *col.* 1. 3 *Hats*. 198.

SEC. XXV.
BILLS, SECOND READING.

THE 2nd reading must regularly be on another day. *Hakew*. 143. It is done by the clerk at the table, who then hands it to the Speaker. The Speaker, rising, states to the house the title of the bill, that this is the 2nd time of reading it, and that the question will be whether it shall be committed, or engrossed and read a 3d time? But if the bill came from the other house, as it always comes engrossed, he states that the question will be whether it shall be read a 3d time? and before he has so reported the state of the bill, no one is to speak to it. *Hakew*. 143. 146.

In the Senate of the United States, the President reports the title of the bill, that this is the 2nd time of reading it, that it is now to be considered as in a committee of the whole, and the question will be whether it shall be read a 3d time? or that it may be referred to a special committee.

SEC. XXVI.
BILLS, COMMITMENT.

IF on motion and question it be decided that the bill shall be committed, it may then be moved to be referred to a committee of the whole house, or to a special committee. If the latter, the Speaker proceeds to name the committee. Any member also may name a single person, and the clerk is to write him down as of the committee. But the house have a controuling power over the names and number, if a question be moved against any one, and may in any case put in and put out whom they please.

Special committee or whole house?

Those who take exceptions to some particulars in the bill are to be of the committee. But none who speak directly against the body of the bill. For he that would totally destroy, will not amend it. *Hakew.* 146. *Town. coll.* 208. *D'Ewes*, 634. *col.* 2. *Scob.* 47. or as is said, 5 *Grey*, 145, the child is not to be put to a nurse that cares not for it. 6 *Grey*, 373. It is

THOMAS JEFFERSON

therefore a constant rule 'that no man is to be employed in any matter who has declared himself against it.' And when any member who is against the bill hears himself named of its committee, he ought to ask to be excused. Thus March 7, 1606, Mr. Hadley was, on the question's being put, excused from being of a committee, declaring himself to be against the matter itself. *Scob.* 46.

No bill shall be committed or amended until it shall have been twice read, after which it may be referred to a committee. *Rule* 14.

All committees shall be appointed by ballot, and a plurality of voices shall make a choice. Rule 15.

The clerk may deliver the bill to any member of the committee. *Town. col.* 138. But it is usual to deliver it to him who is first named.

In some cases, the house has ordered a committee to withdraw immediately into the committee chamber, and act on, and bring back the bill, sitting the house. *Scob.* 48.

A committee meets when and where they please, if the House has not ordered time and place for them. 6. *Grey.* 370. But they can only act when together, and not by separate consultation and consent, nothing being the report of the committee but what has been agreed to in committee actually assembled.

A majority of the committee constitutes a Quorum for business. *Elsynge's
method of passing bills.* 11.

Any member of the House may be
present at any select committee, but cannot vote,
and must give place to all of the committee, and
sit below them. *Elsynge* 12. *Scob.* 49.

The committee have full power over
the bill, or other paper committed to them,
except that they cannot change the title or
subject. 8. *Grey.* 228.

The paper before a committee,
whether select, or of the whole, may be a bill,
resolutions, draught of an address, &c. and
it may either originate with them, or be referred to them. In every case, the whole paper is read first by the clerk, and then by the
chairman by paragraphs. *Scob.* 49. pausing at
the end of each paragraph, and putting
questions for amending, if proposed. In the
case of resolutions on distinct subjects, originating with themselves, a question is put on
each separately, as amended, or unamended,
and no final question on the whole: 3 *Hats.*
276. But if they relate to the same subject, a
question is put on the whole. If it be a bill,
draught of an address, or other paper originating with them, they proceed by para-

Rules for
committees

Amendments

graphs, putting questions for amending, either by insertion or striking out, if proposed: but no question on agreeing to the paragraphs separately. This is reserved to the close, when a question is put on the whole, for agreeing to it as amended, or unamended. But if it be a paper referred to them, they proceed to put questions of amendment, if proposed, but no final question on the whole: because all parts of the paper having been adopted by the House, stand of course, unless altered, or struck out by a vote. Even if they are opposed to the whole paper, and think it cannot be made good by amendments, they cannot reject it, but must report it back to the House without amendments, and there make their opposition.

The natural order in considering and amending any paper is, to begin at the beginning, and proceed through it by paragraphs; and this order is so strictly adhered to in parliament, that when a latter part has been amended, you cannot recur back and make any alteration in a former part. 2 *Hats.* 90. In numerous assemblies this restraint is doubtless important. *But in Senate of the United States though in the main we consider and amend the paragraphs in their natural order, yet recurrences are indulged: and they seem on the whole, in that small body, to produce advantages overweighing their inconveniences.*

To this natural order of beginning at the beginning, there is a single exception found in parliamentary usage. When a bill is taken up in committee, or on its 2nd reading, they postpone the preamble, till the other parts of the bill are gone through. The reason is that on consideration of the body of the bill such alterations may therein be made as may also occasion the alteration of the preamble. *Scob.* 50. 7 *Grey* 431.

Importance of preamble

On this head the following case occurred in Senate, March 6, 1800. A resolution, which had no preamble, having been already amended by the House so that a few words only of the original remained in it, a motion was made to prefix a preamble, which having an aspect very different from the resolution, the mover intimated that he should afterwards propose a correspondent amendment in the body of the resolution. It was objected that a preamble could not be taken up till the body of the resolution is done with. But the preamble was received: because we are in fact through the body of the resolution, we have amended that as far as amendments have been offered, and indeed till little of the original is left. It is the proper time therefore to consider a preamble: and whether the one offered be consistent with the resolution, is for the House to determine. —The mover indeed has intimated that he shall offer a subsequent proposition for the body of the resolution; but the House is not in possession of it; it remains in his breast, and may be withheld. The rules of the House can only operate on what is before them. *The practice of the Senate too allows recurrences backwards and forwards for the purposes of amendment, not permitting amendments in a subsequent, to preclude those in a prior part, or e converso.*

Role of the Committee

When the committee is through the whole, a member moves that the committee may rise and the chairman report the paper to the House, with or without amendments, as the case may be. 2 *Hats.* 289. 292. *Scob.* 53. 2 *Hats.* 290. 8 *Scob.* 50.

When a vote is once passed in a committee, it cannot be altered but by the house, their votes being binding on themselves. 1607, *June* 4.

The committee may not erase, interline, or blot the bill itself; but must in a paper by itself, set down the amendments, stating the words which are to be inserted

or omitted. *Scob.* 50. and where, by references to the page, line and word of the bill.
Scob. 50.

SEC. XXVII.
REPORT OF COMMITTEE.

THE chairman of the committee, standing in
his place, informs the house that the committee, to whom was referred such a bill, have,
according to order, had the same under consideration, and have directed him to report
the same without any amendment, or with
sundry amendments, (as the case may be)
which he is ready to do when the house
pleases to receive it. And he, or any other may
move that it be now received. But the cry of
'now, now,' from the house, generally dispenses with the formality of a motion and
question. He then reads the amendments
with the coherence in the bill, and opens the
alterations, and the reasons of the committee
for such amendments until he has gone
through the whole. He then delivers it at the
clerk's table, where the amendments reported
are read by the clerk, without the coherence,
whereupon the papers lie on the table till the
house at its convenience shall take up the report. *Scob.* 52. *Hakew.* 148.

Committee chairman

The report being made, the committee is dissolved and can act no more without a new power. *Scob.* 51. But it may be revived by a vote, and the same matter recommitted to them. 4 *Grey*, 361.

SEC. XXVIII.
BILL, RECOMMITMENT.

Bills return to the same committee

AFTER a bill has been committed and reported, it ought not, in an ordinary course, to be recommitted. But in cases of importance, and for special reasons, it is sometimes recommitted, and usually to the same committee. *Hakew.* 151. If a report be recommitted before agreed to in the house, what has passed in committee is of no validity; the whole question is again before the committee, and a new resolution must be again moved, as if nothing had passed. 3 *Hats.* 131. *note.*

In Senate, January 1800, the salvage bill was recommitted three times after the commitment.

A particular clause of a bill may be committed without the whole bill, 3 *Hats.* 131. or so much of a paper to one, and so much to another committee.

SEC. XXIX.
BILL, REPORT TAKEN UP.

WHEN the report of a paper originating with a committee is taken up by the house, they proceed exactly as in committee. Here, as in committee, when the paragraphs have, on distinct questions, been agreed to seriatim, 5 *Grey*, 366. 6 *Grey*, 368. 8 *Grey*, 47. 104. 360. 1 *Torbuck's deb.* 125. 3 *Hats.* 348. no question needs be put on the whole report. 5 *Grey*, 381.

Bills with and without amendments

　　On taking up a bill reported with amendments, the amendments only are read by the clerk. The Speaker then reads the first, and puts it to the question, and so on till the whole are adopted or rejected, before any other amendment be admitted, except it be an amendment to an amendment. *Elsynges Mem.* 53. When through the amendments of the committee, the Speaker pauses, and gives time for amendments to be proposed in the house to the body of the bill: as he does also if it has been reported without amendments; putting no questions but on amendments proposed: and when through the whole, he puts the question whether the bill shall be read a 3d time?

SEC. XXX.
QUASI-COMMITTEE.

*How the
U.S. Senate
proceeds*

IF on the motion and question, the bill be not committed, or if no proposition for commitment be made, then the proceedings in the Senate of the United States, and in parliament, are totally different. The former shall be first stated.

The 20th rule of the Senate says, 'All bills, on a 2nd reading, shall first be considered by the Senate in the same manner as if the Senate were in a committee of the whole, before they shall be taken up and proceeded on by the Senate agreeably to the standing rules, unless otherwise ordered:' that is to say unless ordered to be referred to a special committee.

The proceeding of the Senate as in a committee of the whole, or in Quasi-Committee, is precisely as in a real committee of the whole, taking no questions but on amendments. When through the whole, they consider the Quasi-Committee as risen, the house resumed, without any motion, question, or resolution to that effect, and the President reports that 'the house acting as in a committee of the whole, have had under their consideration the bill intituled, &c. and have made sundry amendments which he will now report to the house.' The bill is then before them, as it would have been if reported from a committee, and ques-

tions are regularly to be put again on every amendment: which being gone through, the President pauses to give time to the house to propose amendments to the body of the bill, and when through, puts the question whether it shall be read a 3d time?

After progress in amending a bill in Quasi-Committee a motion may be made to refer it to a Special committee. If the motion prevails, it is equivalent in effect to the several votes that the committee rise, the house resume itself, discharge the committee of the whole, and refer the bill to a special committee. In that case the amendments already made fall. But if the motion fails, the Quasi-Committee stands in statu quo.

Special Committee

How far does this 20th rule subject the house when in Quasi-Committee to the laws which regulate the proceedings of committees of the whole? The particulars in which these differ from proceedings in the house are the following. 1. In a committee every member may speak as often as he pleases. 2. The votes of a committee may be rejected or altered when reported to the house. 3. A committee, even of the whole, cannot refer any matter to another committee. 4. In a committee no previous question can be taken. The only means to avoid an improper discussion is to move that the committee rise: and if it be appre-

Differences in rules for committees and whole house

hended that the same discussion will be attempted on returning into committee, the house can discharge them, and proceed itself on the business, keeping down the improper discussion by the previous question. 5. A committee cannot punish a breach of order, in the house, or in the gallery, 9 *Grey*, 113. It can only rise and report it to the house, who may proceed to punish. *The 1st, and 2d of these peculiarities attach to the Quasi-Committee of the Senate, as every day's practice proves; and seem to be the only ones to which the 20th rule meant to subject them. For it continues to be a house, and therefore though it acts in some respects as a committee, in others it preserves its character as a house. Thus 3. it is in the daily habit of referring its business to a special committee. 4. It admits the Previous Question. If it did not, it would have no means of preventing an improper discussion; not being able as a committee is, to avoid it by returning into the house: for the moment it would resume the same subject there, the 20th rule declares it again a Quasi-Committee. 5. It would doubtless exercise its powers as a house on any breach of order. 6. It takes a question by Yea and Nay, as the house does. 7. It receives messages from the President and the other house. 8. In the midst of a debate it receives a motion to adjourn, and adjourns as a house, not as a committee.*

Application of the 20th rule

SEC. XXXI.
BILL, 2D READING IN THE HOUSE.

IN parliament after the bill has been read a 2d time, if, on the motion and question, it be not committed, or if no proposition for commitment be made, the Speaker reads it by paragraphs, pausing between each, but putting no question but on amendments proposed; and when through the whole, he puts the question whether it shall be read a 3d time? if it came from the other house. Or, if originating with themselves, whether it shall be engrossed and read a 3d time? The Speaker reads sitting, but rises to put questions. The clerk stands while he reads.

But the Senate of the United States is so much in the habit of making many and material amendments at the 3d reading, that it has become the practice not to engross a bill till it has passed. An irregular and dangerous practice; because, in this way, the paper which passes the Senate is not that which goes to the other house; and that which goes to the other house as the act of the Senate, has never been seen in Senate. In reducing numerous, difficult, and illegible amendments into the text, the Secretary may, with the most innocent intentions, commit errors, which can never again be corrected.

The danger of amendments

The time to attach a bill

The bill being now as perfect as its friends can make it, this is the proper stage for those fundamentally opposed, to make their first attack. All attempts at earlier periods are with disjointed efforts; because many who do not expect to be in favor of the bill ultimately, are willing to let it go on to its perfect state, to take time to examine it themselves, and to hear what can be said for it; knowing that, after all, they will have sufficient opportunities of giving it their veto. Its two last stages therefore are reserved for this, that is to say, on the question whether it shall be read a 3d time? And lastly, whether it shall pass? The first of these is usually the most interesting contest; because then the whole subject is new and engaging, and the minds of the members having not yet been declared by any trying vote, the issue is the more doubtful. In this stage therefore, is the main trial of strength between its friends and opponents: and it behoves every one to make up his mind decisively for this question, or he loses the main battle; and accident and management may, and often do, prevent a successful rallying on the next and last question whether it shall pass?

When the bill is engrossed, the title is to be endorsed on the back, and not within the bill. *Hakew.* 250.

SEC. XXXII.
READING PAPERS.

WHERE papers are laid before the house, or referred to a committee, every member has a right to have them once read at the table, before he can be compelled to vote on them. But it is a great, though common error, to suppose that he has a right, toties quoties, to have acts, journals, accounts, or papers on the table read independently of the will of the House. The delay and interruption which this might be made to produce, evince the impossibility of the existence of such a right. There is indeed so manifest a propriety of permitting every member to have as much information as possible on every question on which he is to vote, that when he desires the reading, if it be seen that it is really for information and not for delay, the Speaker directs it to be read without putting a question, if no one objects. But if objected to, a question must be put. 2 *Hats.* 117. 118.

It is equally an error to suppose that any member has a right without a question put, to lay a book or paper on the table, and have it read, on suggesting that it contains matter infringing on the privileges of the house. *ib.*

Rules governing the reading of papers

For the same reason a member has not a right to read a paper in his place, if it be objected to, without leave of the house. But this rigour is never exercised, but where there is an intentional or gross abuse of the time and patience of the House.

A member has not a right even to read his own speech, committed to writing, without leave. This also is to prevent an abuse of time; and therefore is not refused, but where that is intended. 2 *Grey.* 227.

A report of a committee of the Senate on a bill from the House of Representatives, being under consideration, on motion that the report of the committee of the House of Representatives on the same bill be read in Senate, it passed in the negative; Feb. 28. 1793.

Formerly when papers were referred to a committee, they used to be first read: but of late, only the titles; unless a member insists they shall be read, and then no body can oppose it. 2. *Hats.* 117.

SEC. XXXIII.
PRIVILEGED QUESTIONS.

WHILE a question is before the Senate, no motion shall be received unless for an amendment, for the Previous Question, or for postponing the main Question, or to commit it, or to adjourn. *Rule* 8.

It is no possession of a bill unless it be delivered to the clerk to be read, or the Speaker reads the title. *Lex. parl.* 274. *Elsynge mem.* 95. *Ord. House of Commons,* 64.

It is a general rule that the question first moved and seconded shall be first put. *Scob.* 28. 22. 2 *Hats.* 81. But this rule gives way to what may be called Privileged questions; and the Privileged questions are of different grades among themselves.

Priorities

A motion to adjourn simply takes place of all others; for otherwise, the House might be kept sitting against its will, and indefinitely. Yet this motion cannot be received after another question is actually put, and while the House is engaged in voting.

Orders of the day take place of all other questions, except for adjournment. That is to say the question which is the subject of an order is made a privileged one pro hac vice. The order is a repeal of the general rule as to this special case. When any member moves therefore for the orders of the day to be read, no further debate is permitted on the question which was before the house; for if the debate might proceed, it might continue through the day, and defeat the order. This motion, to entitle it to precedence, must be for the orders generally, and not for any particular one; and if it be carried on the question, 'Whether the house will now proceed to the orders of the day,' they must be read and proceeded on in the course in which they stand. 2 *Hats.* 83. For priority of order gives priority of right, which cannot be taken away but by another special order.

After these, there are other privileged questions which will require considerable explanation.

The proper occasion for each question

It is proper that every parliamentary assembly should have certain forms of question so adapted, as to enable them fitly to dispose of every proposition which can be made to them. Such are 1. The Previous Question. 2. To Postpone indefinitely. 3. To adjourn a question to a definite day. 4. To lie on the table. 5. To commit. 6. To amend. The proper occasion for each of these questions should be understood.

The previous question

1. When a proposition is moved, which it is useless or inexpedient now to express or discuss, the previous question has been introduced for suppressing for that time the motion and its discussion. 3. *Hats.* 188. 189.

2. But as the Previous Question gets rid of it only for that day, and the same proposition may recur the next day, if they wish to suppress it for the whole of that session, they postpone it indefinitely. 3. *Hats.* 183. This quashes the proposition for that session, as an indefinite adjournment is a dissolution, or the continuance of a suit sine die is a discontinuance of it. — *To postpone indefinitely*

3. When a motion is made which it will be proper to act on, but information is wanted, or something more pressing claims the present time, the question or debate is adjourned to such day within the session as will answer the views of the House. 2. *Hats.* 81. And those who have spoken before may not speak again when the adjourned debate is resumed. 2. *Hats.* 73. Sometimes however this has been abusively used by adjourning it to a day beyond the session, to get rid of it altogether, as would be done by an indefinite postponement. — *To adjourn a question*

4. When the House has something else which claims its present attention, but would be willing to reserve in their power to take up a proposition whenever it shall suit them, they order it to lie on their table. It may then be called for at any time. — *To lie on the table*

5. If the proposition will want more — *To commit*

amendment and digestion than the formalities of the House will conveniently admit, they refer it to a committee.

To amend

6. But if the proposition be well digested and may need but few and simple amendments, and especially if these be of leading consequence, they then proceed to consider and amend it themselves.

The 8th Rule

The Senate, in their practice, vary from this regular gradation of forms. Their practice, comparatively with that of Parliament stands thus:

For the Parliamentary,		The Senate uses,
Postpmt. indefinite	=	Postp. to a day beyond the session.
Adjournment	=	Postp. to a day within the session.
Lying on the table	=	$\begin{cases} \text{Postpmt. indefinite.} \\ \text{Lying on the table.} \end{cases}$

In their 8th Rule therefore, which declares that while a question is before the Senate, no motion shall be received unless it be for the Previous Question, or to Postpone, Commit, or Amend the Main Question, the term Postponement must be understood according to their broad use of it, and not in its Parliamentary sense. Their rule then establishes as Privileged Questions, the Previous

Question, Postponement, Commitment and Amendment.

But it may be asked, have these questions any privilege among themselves? Or are they so equal that the common principle of the 'first moved, first put' takes place among them? This will need explanation. Their competitions may be as follow:

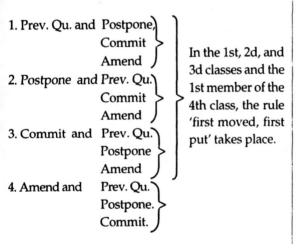

1. Prev. Qu. and Postpone
      Commit
      Amend

2. Postpone and Prev. Qu.
      Commit
      Amend

3. Commit and Prev. Qu.
      Postpone
      Amend

4. Amend and Prev. Qu.
      Postpone.
      Commit.

In the 1st, 2d, and 3d classes and the 1st member of the 4th class, the rule 'first moved, first put' takes place.

Privileges among questions

In the first class where the Previous Question is first moved, the effect is peculiar. For it not only prevents the after motion to postpone or commit from being put to question before it, but also from being put after it. For if the Previous Question be decided affirmatively, to wit, that the Main Question

Classes of questions

1st class shall *now* be put, it would of course be against the decision to postpone or commit. And if it be decided negatively, to wit, that the Main Question shall not now be put, this puts the House out of possession of the Main Question, and consequently there is nothing before them to postpone or commit. So that neither voting for or against the Previous Question, will enable the advocates for postponing or committing to get at their object. Whether it may be amended shall be examined hereafter.

2d class 2d Class. If postponement be decided affirmatively, the proposition is removed from before the house, and consequently there is no ground for the Previous Question commitment, or amendment. But, if decided negatively, that it shall not be postponed, the Main Question may then be suppressed by the Previous Question or may be committed, or amended.

3d class The 3d class is subject to the same observations as the 2d.

4th class The 4th class. Amendment of the Main Question first moved, and afterwards the Previous Question, the question of amendment shall be first put.

Amendment and Postponement competing, Postponement is first put, as the equivalent proposition to adjourn the Main Question would be in parliament. The reason is that the question for amendment is not suppressed by postponing or adjourning the Main Question but remains before the House whenever the Main Question is resumed: and it might be that the occasion for other urgent business might go by, and be lost by length of debate on the amendment, if the House had it not in their power to postpone the whole subject.

Amendment and Postponement

      Amendment and Commitment. The question for committing though last moved shall be first put: because in truth it facilitates and befriends the motion to amend. *Scobell* is express. 'On a motion to amend a bill, any one may notwithstanding move to commit it, and the question for commitment shall be first put.' *Scob.* 46.

Amendment and Commit- ment

      We have hitherto considered the case of two or more of the Privileged questions contending for privilege between themselves, when both were moved on the original or Main Question; but now let us suppose one of them to be moved, not on the original primary question, but on the secondary one, *e.g.*

      Suppose a motion to postpone, commit or amend the Main Question, and that it be moved to suppress that motion by putting a

THOMAS JEFFERSON

Safeguarding a bill

previous question on it. This is not allowed: because it would embarrass questions too much to allow them to be piled on one another several stories high; and the same result may be had in a more simple way, by deciding against the postponement, commitment or amendment. 2 *Hats.* 81, 2, 3, 4.

Suppose a motion for the Previous Question, or commitment, or amendment of the Main Question, and that it be then moved to postpone the motion for the Previous Question, or for commitment or amendment of the Main Question. 1. It would be absurd to postpone the Previous Question, commitment or amendment alone, and thus separate the appendage from its principal. Yet it must be postponed separately from its original, if at all: because the 8th rule of Senate says, that when a Main Question is before the house no motion shall be received but to commit, amend, or pre-question the original question, which is the parliamentary doctrine also. Therefore the motion to postpone the secondary motion for the Previous Question or for committing or amending, cannot be received. 2. This is a piling of questions one on another, which, to avoid embarrassment, is not allowed. 3. The same result may be had more simply, by voting against the Previous Question, commitment or amendment.

Suppose a commitment moved of a motion for the Previous Question, or to postpone or amend. The 1st. 2d. and 3d. reasons before stated all hold good against this.

Suppose an amendment moved to a motion for the Previous Question. Answer. The Previous Question cannot be amended. Parliamentary usage, as well as the 9th rule of the Senate has fixed its form to be 'Shall the Main Question be now put?' *i.e.* at this instant. And as the present instant is but one, it can admit of no modification. To change it to to-morrow, or any other moment, is without example, and without utility. But suppose a motion to amend a motion for postponement; as to one day instead of another, or to a special, instead of indefinite time. The useful character of Amendment gives it a privilege of attaching itself to a secondary and privileged motion. That is, we may amend a postponement of a Main Question. So we may amend a commitment of a Main Question, as by adding, for example, 'with instructions to enquire, &c.' In like manner, if an amendment be moved to an amendment, it is admitted. But it would not be admitted in another degree: to wit, to amend an

9th Rule of the Senate

More on
amendments

amendment to an amendment, of a Main Question. This would lead to too much embarrassment. The line must be drawn somewhere, and usage has drawn it after the amendment to the amendment. The same result must be sought by deciding against the amendment to the amendment, and then moving it again as it was wished to be amended. In this form it becomes only an amendment to an amendment.

The 18th
Rule
of the
Senate

In filling a blank with a sum, the largest sum shall be first put to the question by the 18th rule of the Senate, contrary to the rule of parliament which privileges the smallest sum and longest time. 5 *Grey.* 179. 2 *Hats.* 81. 83. 3 *Hats.* 132. 133. And this is considered to be not in the form of an amendment to the question; but as alternative, or successive originals. In all cases of time or number, we must consider whether the larger comprehends the lesser, as in a question to what day a postponement shall be, the number of a committee, amount of a fine, term of an imprisonment, term of irredeemability of a loan, or the terminus in quem, in any other case. Then the question must begin a maximo. Or whether the lesser concludes the greater, as in questions on the limitation of the rate of interest, on what day the session shall be closed by adjournment, on what day the next shall commence, when an act shall commence, or the terminus a quo in any other case, where the question must begin a minimo. The object being not to begin at that extreme, which, and more, being within every man's wish, no one could negative it, and yet, if he should vote in the affirmative, every question for more would be precluded: but at that extreme which would unite few, and then to advance or recede, till you get to a number which will unite a bare majority. 3 *Grey*, 376, 384, 385. 'The fair question in this case is not that to which and more all will agree, but whether there shall be addition to the question.' 1 *Grey*. 365.

Another exception to the rule of priority is, when a motion has been made to strike out, or agree to a paragraph. Motions to amend it are to be put to the question before a vote is taken on striking out, or agreeing to the whole paragraph.

Another exception

But there are several questions, which being incidental to every one, will take place of every one, privileged or not; to wit, a question of order arising out of any other question, must be decided before that question. 2 *Hats*. 88.

A matter of privilege arising out of any question, or from a quarrel between two members, or any other cause, supersedes the consideration of the original question, and must be first disposed of. 2 *Hats.* 88.

Reading papers relative to the question before the *House*. This question must be put before the principal one. 2 *Hats.* 88.

Leave asked to withdraw a motion. The rule of parliament being, that a motion made and seconded is in possession of the House, and cannot be withdrawn without leave, the very terms of the rule imply that leave may be given, and consequently may be asked and put to the question.

XXXIV.
THE PREVIOUS QUESTION.

WHEN any question is before the House, any member may move a Previous Question 'Whether that question (called the Main Question) shall now be put?' If it pass in the affirmative, then the Main Question is to be put immediately, and no man may speak any thing further to it, either to add or alter. *Memor.* in *Hakew*, 28, 4. *Grey.* 27.

The Previous Question being moved and seconded, the question from the chair shall be, 'Shall the Main Question be now put?' and if the Nays prevail, the

Main Question shall not then be put. *Rule* 9.

This kind of question is understood by Mr. Hatsell to have been introduced in 1604, 2 *Hats.* 80. Sir Henry Vane introduced it. 2 *Grey* 113, 114. 3 *Grey* 384. When the question was put in this form, 'Shall the Main Question be put?' a determination in the negative suppressed the Main Question during the session; but since the words 'now put' are used, they exclude it for the present only. Formerly indeed only till the present debate was over. 4 *Grey.* 43. but now for that day and no longer. 2 *Grey,* 113, 114.

Before the question 'whether the Main Question shall now be put?' any person might formerly have spoken to the Main Question, because otherwise he would be precluded from speaking to it at all. *Mem.* in *Hakew.* 28.

The proper occasion for the Previous Question is when a subject is brought forward of a delicate nature as to high personages, &c. or the discussion of which may call forth observations, which might be of injurious consequences. Then the Previous Question is proposed: and, in the modern usage, the discussion of the Main Question is suspended, and the debate confined to the Previous Question. The use of it has been ex-

Relation to Main Question

Proper Occasion

tended abusively to other cases: but in these
it is an embarrassing procedure: its uses
would be as well answered by other more
simple parliamentary forms, and therefore it
should not be favoured, but restricted within
as narrow limits as possible.

Is amendment possible?

Whether a Main Question may be
amended after the Previous Question on it
has been moved and seconded? 2 *Hats.* 88,
says, if the Previous Question has been
moved and seconded, and also proposed
from the chair, (by which he means stated by
the Speaker for debate) it has been doubted
whether an amendment can be admitted to
the Main Question? He thinks it may, after
the Previous Question moved and seconded;
but not after it has been proposed from the
chair. In this case he thinks the friends to the
amendment must vote that the Main Question be not now put; and then move their
amended question, which being made new
by the amendment, is no longer the same
which has been just suppressed, and therefore may be proposed as a new one. But this
proceeding certainly endangers the Main
Question by dividing its friends, some of
whom may chuse it unamended, rather than
lose it altogether: while others of them may

vote, as Hatsell advises, that the Main Question be not now put, with a view to move it again in an amended form. The enemies to the Main Question, by this manoeuvre of the Previous Question, get the enemies to the amendment added to them on the first vote, and throw the friends of the Main Question under the embarrassment of rallying again as they can. To support his opinion too, he makes the deciding circumstance, whether an amendment may or may not be made, to be that the Previous Question has been proposed from the chair. But as the rule is that the House is in possession of a question as soon as it is moved and seconded, it cannot be more than possessed of it by its being also proposed from the chair. It may be said indeed that the object of the Previous Question being to get rid of a question, which it is not expedient should be discussed, this object may be defeated by moving to amend, and, in the discussion of that motion, involving the subject of the Main Question. But so may the object of the Previous Question be defeated by moving the amended question, as Mr. Hatsell proposes, after the decision against putting the original question. He acknowledges too that the practice has been to admit

Enemies abound

Back to the
Main
Question

previous amendment, and only cites a few late instances to the contrary. On the whole I should think it best to decide it ab inconvenienti, to wit, which is most inconvenient, to put it in the power of one side of the House to defeat a proposition by hastily moving the Previous Question, and thus forcing the Main Question to be put unamended; or to put in the power of the other side to force on, incidentally at least, a discussion which would be better avoided? Perhaps the last is the least inconvenience; inasmuch as the Speaker, by confining the discussion rigorously to the amendment only, may prevent their going into the Main Question, and inasmuch also as so great a proportion of the cases in which the Previous Question is called for, are fair and proper subjects of public discussion, and ought not to be obstructed by a formality introduced for questions of a peculiar character.

SEC. XXXV.
AMENDMENTS.

ON an amendment being moved, a member who has spoken to the main question may speak again to the amendment. *Scob.* 23.

If an amendment be proposed inconsistent with one already agreed to, it is a fit ground for its rejection by the House; but not within the competence of the Speaker to suppress as if it were against order. For were he permitted to draw questions of consistence within the vortex of order, he might usurp a negative on important modifications, and suppress, instead of subserving, the legislative will.

Amendments must also be addressed

Amendments may be made so as totally to alter the nature of the proposition; and it is a way of getting rid of a proposition, by making it bear a sense different from what was intended by the movers, so that they vote against it themselves. 2 *Hats.* 79, 4, 82, 84. A new bill may be ingrafted by way of amendment, on the words 'Be it enacted, &c.' 1 *Grey.* 190, 192.

Ways of amending

If it be proposed to amend by leaving out certain words, it may be moved as an amendment to this amendment to leave out a part of the words of the amendment, which is equivalent to leaving them in the bill. 2 *Hats.* 80, 9. The Parliamentary question is always whether the words shall stand part of the bill?

When it is proposed to amend by inserting a paragraph or part of one, the friends of the paragraph may make it as perfect as they can by amendments, before the question is put for inserting it. If it be received, it cannot be

Different ways of amending

amended afterwards, in the same stage; because the House, has on a vote, agreed to it in that form. In like manner if it is proposed to amend by striking out a paragraph, the friends of the paragraph are first to make it as perfect as they can by amendments, before the question is put for striking it out. If on the question it be retained, it cannot be amended afterwards: because a vote against striking out is equivalent to a vote agreeing to it in that form.

When it is moved to amend, by striking out certain words, and inserting others, the manner of stating the question is first to read the whole passage to be amended as it stands at present, then the words proposed to be struck out, next those to be inserted, and lastly, the whole passage as it will be when amended. And the question, if desired, is then to be divided, and put first on striking out. If carried, it is next on inserting the words proposed. If that be lost, it may be moved to insert others, 2 *Hats.* 80. 7.

A motion is made to amend by striking out certain words, and inserting others in their place, which is negatived. Then it is moved to strike out the same words, and to insert others of a tenor entirely different from those first proposed. It is negatived. Then it is moved to strike out the same words and insert nothing, which is agreed to. All this is admissible; because to strike out and insert A, is one proposition. To strike out and insert B, is a different proposition. And to strike out and insert nothing is still different. And the rejection of one proposition does not preclude the offering a different one. Nor would it change the case were the first motion divided, by putting the question first on striking out, and that negatived. For as putting the whole motion to the question at once, would not have precluded, the putting the half of it cannot do it.*

    But if it had been carried affirmatively to strike out the words and to insert A, it could not afterwards be permitted to strike out A and insert B. The mover of B, should

Amending by striking out certain words

*In the case of a division of the question and a decision against striking out, I advance doubtingly the opinion here expressed. I find no authority either way; and I know it may be viewed under a different aspect. It may be thought that having decided separately not to strike out the passage, the same question for striking out cannot be put over again, though with a view to a different insertion. Still I think it more reasonable and convenient, to consider the striking out and insertion, as forming one proposition; but should readily yield to any evidence that the contrary is the practice in parliament.

have notified while the insertion of A, was under debate, that he would move to insert B. In which case those who preferred it would join in rejecting A.

After A is inserted, however, it may be moved to strike out a portion of the original paragraph, comprehending A, provided the coherence to be struck out be so substantial as to make this effectively a different proposition. For then it is resolved into the common case of striking out a paragraph after amending it. Nor does any thing forbid a new insertion, instead of A and its coherence.

Two motions and two questions

In Senate, January 25, 1798, a motion to postpone until the 2d Tuesday in February some amendments proposed to the constitution. The words 'until the 2d Tuesday in February,' were struck out by way of amendment. Then it was moved, to add 'until the 1st day of June.' Objected that it was not in order, as the question should be first put on the longest time; therefore, after a shorter time decided against, a longer cannot be put to question. It was answered, that this rule takes place only in filling blanks for time. But when a specific time stands part of a motion, that may be struck out as well as any other part of the motion; and when struck out, a motion may be received to insert any other. In fact, it is not till they are struck out, and a blank for the time thereby produced, that the rule can begin to operate, by receiving all the propositions for different times, and putting the questions successively on the longest. Otherwise, it would be in the power of the mover, by inserting originally a short time, to preclude the possibility of a longer. For till the short time is struck out, you cannot insert a longer; and if, after it is struck out, you cannot do it, then it cannot be done at all. —Suppose the first motion had been to amend by striking out 'the 2d Tuesday of February,' and inserting instead thereof 'the 1st of June.' It would have been regular then to divide the question, by proposing first the question to strike out, and then that to insert. Now this is precisely the effect of the present proceeding; only instead of one motion and two questions, there are two motions and two questions, to effect it; the motion being divided as well as the question.

When the matter contained in two bills might be better put into one, the manner is to reject the one, and incorporate its matter into another bill by way of amendment. So if the matter of one bill would be better distributed into two, any part may be

Consolidating bills

struck out by way of amendment, and put into a new bill. If a section is to be transposed, a question must be put on striking it out where it stands, and another for inserting it in the place desired.

A bill passed by the one house with blanks. These may be filled up by the other; by way of amendments, returned to the first as such and passed. 3 *Hats.* 83.

The number prefixed to the section of a bill, being merely a marginal indication, and no part of the text of the bill, the clerk regulates that, the house or committee is only to amend the text.

SEC. XXXVI.
DIVISION OF THE QUESTION.

A complicated question may be divided

IF a question contain more parts than one, it may be divided into two or more questions. *Mem.* in *Hakew.* 29. But not as the right of an individual member, but with the consent of the house. For who is to decide whether a question is complicated or not? where it is complicated? into how many propositions it may be divided? The fact is, that the only mode of separating a complicated question is by moving amendments to it; and these must be decided by the House on a question: unless the House orders it to be divided: as on the question December 2, 1640, making void the election of the knights for Worcester, on a motion it was resolved, to make two questions of it, to wit, one on each knight. 2 *Hats.* 85, 86. So wherever there are several names in a question, they may be divided and put one by one. 9 *Grey.* 444. So 1729, April 17, on an objection that a question was complicated, it was separated by amendment. 2 *Hats.* 79, 5.

The soundness of these observations will be evident from the embarrassments produced by the 10th rule of the Senate, which says, 'if the question in debate contain several points, any member may have the same divided.'

10th Rule of the Senate

1798, May 30, the Alien Bill in Quasi-committee. To a section and Proviso in the original, had been added two new Provisoes by way of amendment. On a motion to strike out the section as amended, the question was desired to be divided. To do this it must be put first on striking out either the former Proviso, or some distinct member of the section. But when nothing remains but the last member of the section, and the Provisoes, they cannot be divided so as to put the last member to question by itself; for the Provisoes might thus be left standing alone as ex-

The Alien Bill is an example

ceptions to a rule when the rule is taken away; or the new Provisoes might be left to a second question, after having been decided on once before at the same reading; which is contrary to rule. But the question must be on striking out the last member of the section as amended. This sweeps away the exceptions with the rule, and relieves from inconsistence. A question to be divisible, must comprehend points so distinct and entire, that one of them being taken away, the other may stand entire. But a Proviso or exception, without an enacting clause, does not contain an entire point or proposition.

Parts of a question must be able to stand alone

May 31. The same bill being before the Senate. There was a proviso that the bill should not extend, 1. To any foreign minister; nor, 2. to any person to whom the President should give a passport; nor, 3. to any alien merchant conforming himself to such regulations as the President shall prescribe, and a division of the question into its simplest elements was called for. It was divided into 4 parts, the 4th taking in the words 'conforming himself, &c.' It was objected that the words 'any alien merchant,' could not be separated from their modifying words 'conforming, &c.' because these words, if left by themselves, contain no substantive idea, will make no sense. But admitting that the divisions of a paragraph into separate questions must be so made as that each part may stand by itself, yet the house having, on the question, retained the two first divisions, the words 'any alien merchant' may be struck out, and their modifying words will then attach themselves to the preceding description of persons, and become a modification of that description.

When a question is divided, after the question on the 1st member, the 2d is open to debate and amendment: because it is a known rule that a person may rise and speak at any time before the question has been completely decided, by putting the negative, as well as affirmative side. But the question is not completely put, when the vote has been taken on the first member only. One half of the question, both affirmative and negative, remains still to be put. See *Execut. Journ. June 25, 1795.* The same decision by President Adams.

*All parts
are open
to debate*

SEC. XXXVII.
CO-EXISTING QUESTIONS.

IT may be asked whether the House can be in possession of two motions or propositions at the same time? So that, one of them being

Only Privileged Questions can co-exist

decided, the other goes to question without being moved anew? The answer must be special. When a question is interrupted by a vote of adjournment, it is thereby removed from before the House, and does not stand ipso facto before them at their next meeting: but must come forward in the usual way. So, when it is interrupted by the order of the day. Such other privileged questions also as dispose of the main question (e.g. the previous question, postponement or commitment) remove it from before the house. But it is only suspended by a motion to amend, to withdraw, to read papers, or, by a question of order or privilege, and stands again before the House when these are decided. None but the class of privileged questions can be brought forward, while there is another question before the House, the rule being that when a motion has been made and seconded, no other can be received, except it be a privileged one.

SEC. XXXVIII.
EQUIVALENT QUESTIONS.

IF, on a question for rejection, a bill be retained, it passes of course to its next reading. *Hakew.* 141. *Scob.* 42. And a question for a second reading, determined negatively, is a rejection without farther question. 4 *Grey* 149. And see *Elsynge's memor.* 42. in what cases questions are to be taken for rejection.

Where questions are perfectly equivalent, so that the negative of the one amounts to the affirmative of the other, and leaves no other alternative, the decision of the one concludes necessarily the other. 4 *Grey*, 157. Thus the negative of striking out amounts to the affirmative of agreeing; and therefore, to put a question on agreeing after that on striking out, would be to put the same question in effect twice over. Not so in questions of amendments between the two houses. A motion to recede being negatived, does not amount to a positive vote to insist, because there is another alternative, to wit, to adhere.

Two sides of the same question

A bill originating in one House, is passed by the other with an amendment. A motion in the originating House to agree to the amendment is negatived. Does there result from this a vote of disagreement, or must the question on disagreement be expressly voted? The questions respecting amendments from another house are, 1st. To agree. 2d disagree. 3d recede. 4th insist. 5th adhere.

1st. To agree. 2d. To disagree.	Either of these concludes the other necessarily: for the positive of either is exactly the equivalent of the negative of the other, and no other alternative remains. On either motion amendments to the amendment may be proposed, e.g. if it be moved to disagree, those who are for the amendment have a right to propose amendments, and to make it as perfect as they can, before the question of disagreeing is put.
3d. To recede. You may then either insist or adhere. 4th. To insist. You may then either recede or adhere. 5th. To adhere. You may then either recede or insist.	Consequently the negative of these is not equivalent to a positive vote the other way. It does not raise so necessary an implication as may authorise the Secretary by inference to enter another vote: for two alternatives still remain, either of which may be adopted by the house.

SEC. XXXIX.
THE QUESTION.

THE question is to be put first on the affirmative, and then on the negative side.

    After the Speaker has put the affirmative part of the question, any member who has not spoken before to the question, may rise and speak before the negative be put. Because it is no full question till the negative part be put. *Scob.* 23, 2 *Hats.* 73.

Affirmative arguments precede negative

    But in small matters, and which are of course, such as receiving petitions, reports, withdrawing motions, reading papers, &c. the Speaker most commonly supposes the consent of the house, where no objection is expressed, and does not give them the trouble of putting the question formally. *Scob.* 22. 2 *Hats.* 79. 2. 87. 5 *Grey.* 129. 9 *Grey.* 301.

SEC. XL.
BILLS, THIRD READING.

TO prevent bills from being passed by surprise, the house by a standing order directs that they shall not be put on their passage before a fixed hour, naming one at which the house is commonly full. *Hakew.* 153.

The usage of the Senate is not to put bills on their passage till noon.

A bill reported and passed to the 3d reading cannot on that day be read the 3d time and passed. Because this would be to pass on two readings in the same day.

Announcing the 3d reading

At the 3d reading, the clerk reads the bill and delivers it to the Speaker, who states the title, that it is the 3d time of reading the bill, and that the question will be whether it shall pass? Formerly the Speaker or those who prepared a bill, prepared also a breviate or summary statement of its contents, which the Speaker read when he declared the state of the bill, at the several readings. Sometimes however, he read the bill itself, especially on its passage. *Hakew.* 136. 137. 153. *Coke,* 22. 115. Latterly, instead of this, he, at the third reading, states the whole contents of the bill verbatim, only instead of reading the formal parts, 'Be it enacted, &c.' he states that 'the preamble recites so and so—the 1st section enacts that, &c. the 2d section enacts, &c.'

Senate practices differ

But in the Senate of the United States, both of these formalities are dispensed with; the Breviate presenting but an imperfect view of the Bill, and being capable of being made to present a false one: and the full statement being an useless waste of time, immediately after a full reading by the clerk; and especially as every member has a printed copy in his hand.

A bill on the 3d reading is not to be committed for the matter or body thereof; but to receive some particular clause or proviso, it hath been sometimes suffered, but as a thing very unusual. *Hakew.* 156. thus 27 *El.* 1584. a bill was committed on the 3d reading, having been formerly committed on the 2d, but is declared not usual. *D'Ewes* 337. *col.* 2, 414. *col.* 2.

When an essential provision has been omitted, rather than erase the bill, and render it suspicious, they add a clause on a separate paper, engrossed and called a Ryder, which is read and put to the question three times. *Elsynge's memorials* 59. 6 *Grey,* 335. 1 *Blackst.* 183. For examples of Ryders see 3 *Hats.* 121. 122. 124. 126. Every one is at liberty to bring in a Ryder without asking leave. 10 *Grey,* 52.

About Ryders

It is laid down as a general rule that amendments proposed at the 2d reading shall be twice read, and those proposed at the 3d reading thrice read; as also all amendments from the other house. *Town. col.* 19. 23. 24. 25. 26. 27. 28.

It is with great, and almost invincible reluctance, that amendments are admitted at this reading, which occasion erasures or interlineations. Sometimes a proviso has been cut off from a bill; sometimes erased. 9 *Grey*, 513.

Importance of 3d reading

This is the proper stage for filling up blanks; for if filled up before, and now altered by erasure, it would be peculiarly unsafe.

At his reading the bill is debated afresh, and for the most part is more spoken to, at this time, than on any of the former readings. *Hakew.* 153.

The debate on the question whether it should be read a 3d time? has discovered to its friends and opponents the arguments on which each side relies, and which of these appear to have influence with the house; they have had time to meet them with new arguments, and to put their old ones into new shapes. The former vote has tried the strength of the first opinion and furnished grounds to estimate the issue; and the question now offered for its passage, is the last occasion which is ever to be offered for carrying or rejecting it.

When the debate is ended, the Speaker, holding the bill in his hand, puts the question for its passage, by saying, 'Gentlemen, all you who are of opinion that this bill shall pass, say aye,' and after the answer of the ayes, 'All those of the contrary opinion say no.' *Hakew.* 154.

After the bill is passed, there can be no further alteration of it in any point. *Hakew.* 159.

SEC. XLI.
DIVISION OF THE HOUSE.

THE affirmative and negative of the question having been both put and answered, the Speaker declares whether the Yeas or Nays have it by the sound, if he be himself satisfied, and it stands as the judgment of the house. But if he be not himself satisfied which voice is the greater, or if, before any other member comes into the house, or before any new motion made (for it is too late after that) any member shall rise and declare himself dissatisfied with the Speaker's decision, then the Speaker is to divide the house. *Scob.* 24. 2 *Hats.* 140.

The Speaker divides the house

When the house of commons is divided, the one party goes forth, and the other remains in the house. This has made it important which go forth, and which remain; because the latter gain all the indolent, the indifferent and inattentive. Their general rule therefore is, that those who give their votes for the preservation of the orders of the house, shall stay in, and those who are for introducing any new matter or

Who goes, who stays?

alteration, or proceeding contrary to the established course, are to go out. But this rule is subject to many exceptions and modifications. 2 *Hats.* 134. 1 *Rush. p.* 3, *fol.* 92. *Scob.* 43, 52. *Co.* 12, 116. *D'Ewes.* 505. *col.* 1. *Mem.* in *Hakew.* 25, 29, as will appear by the following statement of who go forth.

Petition that it be received* Read	Ayes.
Lie on the table Rejected after refusal to lie on table	Noes.
Referred to a committee or farther proceeding	Ayes.
Bill, that it be brought in Read 1st or 2d time Engrossed, or read 3d time Proceeding on every other stage Committed	Ayes.
To committee of the whole	Noes.
To a select committee	Ayes.
Report of bill to lie on table	Noes.
Be *now* read Be taken into consideration 3 months hence	Ayes. 30 P.J.251.
Amendments be read a 2d time	Noes.
Clause offered on report of bill be read 2d time For receiving a clause With amendments be engrossed	Ayes. 334. 395.
That a bill be now read a 3d time	Noes. 398.

*Noes. 9 *Grey* 365.

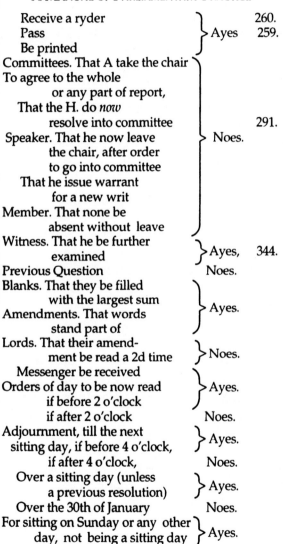

Receive a ryder ⎫ 260.
Pass ⎬ Ayes 259.
Be printed ⎭

Committees. That A take the chair ⎫
To agree to the whole
 or any part of report,
 That the H. do *now*
  resolve into committee ⎬ 291.
Speaker. That he now leave Noes.
 the chair, after order
 to go into committee
 That he issue warrant
  for a new writ
Member. That none be
 absent without leave ⎭

Witness. That he be further ⎫ Ayes, 344.
 examined ⎭
Previous Question Noes.

Blanks. That they be filled ⎫
 with the largest sum
Amendments. That words ⎬ Ayes.
 stand part of ⎭

Lords. That their amend- ⎫ Noes.
 ment be read a 2d time ⎭

Messenger be received ⎫
Orders of day to be now read ⎬ Ayes.
 if before 2 o'clock ⎭
 if after 2 o'clock Noes.

Adjournment, till the next ⎫ Ayes.
 sitting day, if before 4 o'clock, ⎭
 if after 4 o'clock, Noes.

Over a sitting day (unless ⎫ Ayes.
 a previous resolution) ⎭
Over the 30th of January Noes.

For sitting on Sunday or any other ⎫ Ayes.
 day, not being a sitting day ⎭

*The procedure,
past and
present*

The one party being gone forth, the Speaker names two tellers from the affirmative, and two from the negative side, who first count those sitting in the House, and report the number to the Speaker. Then they place themselves within the door, two on each side, and count those who went forth, as they come in, and report the number to the Speaker. *Mem.* in *Hakew.* 26.

A mistake in the report of the tellers may be rectified after the report made. 2 *Hats.* 145. note.

But in both houses of Congress all these intricacies are avoided. The Ayes first rise and are counted, standing in their places, by the President or Speaker. Then they sit, and the Noes rise and are counted in like manner.

In Senate, if they be equally divided, the Vice president announces his opinion, which decides.

The constitution however has directed that 'the Yeas and Nays of the members of either house on any question shall, at the desire of one fifth of those present, be entered on the Journal.' And again, that in all cases of reconsidering a bill, disapproved by the President, and returned with his objections, 'the votes of both houses shall be determined by Yeas and Nays, and the names of the persons voting for and against the bill, shall be entered on the journals of each house respectively.'

By the 11th rule of the Senate, when the Yeas and Nays shall be called for by one fifth of the members present, each member called upon, shall, unless for special reasons he be excused by the Senate, declare openly and without debate, his assent or dissent to the question. In taking the Yeas and Nays, and upon the call of the house, the names of the members shall be taken alphabetically.

When it is proposed to take the vote by Yeas and Nays, the President or Speaker states that 'the Question is whether e.g. the bill shall pass? that it is proposed that the Yeas and Nays shall be entered on the journal. Those therefore who desire it will rise.' If he finds and declares that one fifth have risen, he then states that 'those who are of opinion that the bill shall pass are to answer in the affirmative, those of the contrary opinion in the negative.' The clerk then calls over the names alphabetically, notes the Yea or Nay of each, and gives the list to the President or Speaker, who declares the result. In Senate, if there be an equal division, the secretary calls on the Vice president, and notes his affirmative or negative, which becomes the decision of the house.

The 11th Senate Rule

In the House of Commons, every member must give his vote the one way or the other. *Scob.* 24. As it is not permitted to

Only one vote on a question

any one to withdraw who is in the House when the question is put, nor is any one to be told in the division who was not in when the question was put. 2 *Hats.* 140.

This last position is always true when the vote is by Yeas and Nays; where the Negative as well as Affirmative of the question is stated by the President at he same time, and the vote of both sides begins and proceeds pari passu. It is true also when the question is put in the usual way, if the negative has also been put. But if it has not, the member entering, or any other member may speak, and even propose amendments, by which the debate may be opened again, and the question be greatly deferred. And as some who have answered Aye, may have been changed by the new arguments, the Affirmative must be put over again. If then the member entering may, by speaking a few words, occasion a repetition of the question, it would be useless to deny it on his simple call for it.

While the house is telling, no member may speak, or move out of his place; for it any mistake be suspected, it must be told again. *Mem.* in *Hakew.* 26. 2 *Hats.* 143.

If any difficulty arises in point of order during the division, the Speaker is to decide peremptorily, subject to the future censure of the House if irregular. He sometimes permits old experienced members to assist him with their advice, which they do, sitting in their seats, covered, to avoid the appearance of debate; but this can only be with the Speaker's leave, else the division might last several hours. 2 *Hats.* 143.

The Speaker's role reviewed

The voice of the majority decides. For the lex majoris partis is the law of all councils, elections, &c. where not otherwise expressly provided. *Hakew.* 93. But if the house be equally divided, 'semper presumatur pro negante:' that is, the former law is not to be changed but by a majority. *Towns. col.* 134.

But in the Senate of the United States, the Vice President decides, when the house is divided. Constitution United States I. 3.

When from counting the House on a division, it appears that there is not a quorum, the matter continues exactly in the state in which it was before the division, and must be resumed at that point on any future day. 2 *Hats.* 126.

1606, May 1, on a question whether a member having said Yea, may afterwards sit and change his opinion? a precedent was remembered by the Speaker, of Mr. Morris, attorney of the wards in 39 *Eliz.* who in like case changed his opinion. *Mem.* in *Hakew.* 27.

SEC. XLII.
TITLE.

AFTER the Bill has passed, and not before, the Title may be amended, and is to be fixed by a question; and the Bill is then sent to the other House.

SEC. XLIII.
RECONSIDERATION.

How a bill can be reconsidered

WHEN *a question has been once made and carried in the affirmative, or negative, it shall be in order for any member of the majority, to move for the reconsideration thereof.* Rule 22.

1798, January. A bill on its 2d reading, being amended, and on the question whether it shall be read a 3d time negatived, was restored by a decision to reconsider that question. Here the votes of negative and reconsideration, like positive and negative quantities in equation, destroy one another, and are as if they were expunged from the journals. Consequently the bill is open for amendment, just so far as it was the moment preceding the question for the 3d reading. That is to say, all parts of the bill are open for amendment, except those on which votes have been already taken in its present stage. So also it may be recommitted.

The rule permitting a reconsideration of a question affixing to it no limitation of time or circumstance, it may be asked whether there is no limitation? If, after the vote, the paper on which it is passed has been parted with, there can be no reconsideration: as if a vote has been for the passage of a bill, and the bill has been sent to the other house. But where the paper remains, as on a bill rejected; when, or under what circumstances does it cease to be susceptible of reconsideration? This remains to be settled; unless a sense that the right of reconsideration is a right to waste the time of the house in repeated agitations of the same question, so that it shall never know when a question is done with, should induce them to reform this anomalous proceeding.

Some problems with this rule

In Parliament, a question once carried, cannot be questioned again at the same session; but must stand as the judgment of the House. *Towns. col.* 67. *Mem.* in *Hakew.* 33. And a Bill once rejected, another of the same substance cannot be brought in again the same session. *Hakew.* 158. 6 *Grey*, 392. But this does not extend to prevent putting the same question in different stages of a bill; because every stage of a bill submits the whole and ev-

Resubmitting bills

ery part of it to the opinion of the House, as open for amendment, either by insertion or omission, though the same amendment has been accepted or rejected in a former stage. So in reports of committees, e.g. report of an address, the same question is before the House, and open for free discussion. *Towns. col.* 26. 2 *Hats.* 98, 100, 101. So orders of the House, or instructions to committees may be discharged. So a bill, begun in one House, sent to the other, and there rejected, may be renewed again in that other, passed and sent back. *Ib.* 92. 3 *Hats.* 161. Or if, instead of being rejected, they read it once and lay it aside, or amend it, and put it off a month, they may order in another to the same effect, with the same or a different title. *Hakew.* 97, 98.

Efforts at improvement

Divers expedients are used to correct the effects of this rule; as by passing an explanatory act, if any thing has been omitted or ill expressed, 3 *Hats.* 278. or an act to enforce, and make more effectual an act, &c. or to rectify mistakes in an act, &c. or a committee on one bill may be instructed to receive a clause to rectify the mistakes of another. Thus, June 24, 1685, a clause was inserted in a bill for rectifying a mistake committed by a clerk in engrossing a bill of supply. 2 *Hats.* 194, 6. Or the session may be closed for one, two, three or more days, and a new one commenced. But then all matters depending must be finished, or they fall, and are to begin de novo. 2 *Hats.* 94, to 98. Or a part of the subject may be taken up by another bill, or taken up in a different way. 6 *Grey.* 304, 316.

And in cases of the last magnitude, this rule has not been so strictly and verbally observed as to stop indispensable proceedings altogether. 2 *Hats.* 92, 98. Thus when the address on the preliminaries of peace in 1782, had been lost by a majority of one, on account of the importance of the question, and smallness of the majority, the same question in substance though with some words not in the first, and which might change the opinion of some members, was brought on again and carried; as the motives for it were thought to outweigh the objection of form. 2 *Hats.* 99, 100.

A case in point

A second bill may be passed to continue an act of the same session; or to enlarge the time limited for its execution. 2 *Hats.* 95, 98. This is not in contradiction to the first act.

SEC. XLIV.
BILLS SENT TO THE OTHER HOUSE.

ALL bills passed in Senate shall, before they are sent to the House of Representatives, be examined by the committees respectively, who brought in

THOMAS JEFFERSON

such bills, or to whom the same have been last committed in Senate. Rule 23.

A bill from the other house is sometimes ordered to lie on the table. 2 *Hats.* 97.

Further clarification sometimes necessary

When bills passed in one House and sent to the other, are grounded on special facts requiring proof, it is usual either by message, or at a conference, to ask the grounds and evidence; and this evidence, whether arising out of papers, or from the examination of witnesses, is immediately communicated. 3 *Hats.* 48.

SEC. XLV.
AMENDMENTS BETWEEN THE HOUSES.

WHEN either House, e.g. the House of Commons, sends a bill to the other, the other may pass it with amendments. The regular progression in this case is that the Commons disagree to the amendment; the Lords insist on it; the Commons insist on their disagreement; the Lords adhere to their amendment; the Commons adhere to their disagreement. The term of insisting may be repeated as often as they choose, to keep the question open. But the first adherence by either renders it necessary for the other to recede or adhere also; when the matter is usually suffered to fall. 10 *Grey*, 148. Latterly however there are instances of their having gone to a second adherence. There must be an absolute conclusion of the subject somewhere, or otherwise transactions between the Houses would become endless. 3 *Hats*. 268, 270. The term of insisting, we are told by Sir John Trevor, was then [1679] newly introduced into parliamentary usage, by the lords. 7 *Grey*, 94. It was certainly a happy innovation, as it multiplies the opportunities of trying modifications which may bring the houses to a concurrence. Either house however is free to pass over the term of insisting, and to adhere in the first instance. 10 *Grey*, 146. But it is not respectful to the other. In the ordinary parliamentary course, there are two free conferences at least before an adherence, 10 *Grey*. 147

To avoid endless transactions

Either house may recede from its amendment and agree to the bill; or recede from their disagreement to the amendment, and agree to the same absolutely, or with an amendment. For here the disagreement and receding destroy one another, and the subject stands as before the disagreement. *Elsynge* 23—27. 9 *Grey*. 476.

But the House cannot recede from, or insist on its own amendment, with an

*Changes
must
stop
somewhere*

amendment: for the same reason that it cannot send to the other House an amendment to its own act after it has passed the act. They may modify an amendment from the other House by ingrafting an amendment on it, because they have never assented to it; but they cannot amend their own amendment, because they have, on the question, passed it in that form. 9 *Grey* 353, 10 *Grey*, 240. In Senate, March 29, 1798. Nor where one house has adhered to their amendment, and the other agrees with an amendment, can the first House depart from the form which they have fixed by an adherence.

In the case of a money bill the lords proposed amendments, become, by delay, confessedly necessary. The Commons however refused them as infringing on their privilege as to money bills; but they offered themselves to add to the bill a proviso to the same effect, which had no coherence with the Lords' amendments; and urged that it was an expedient warranted by precedent, and not unparliamentary in a case become impracticable and irremediable in any other way. 3 *Hats.* 256. 266. 270. 271. But the Lords refused, and the bill was lost. 1 *Chand.* 288. A like case, 1 *Chand.* 311. —So the Commons resolve that it is unparliamentary to strike out at a conference any thing in a bill which hath been agreed and passed by both Houses. 6 *Grey*, 274. 1 *Chand*. 312.

A motion to amend an amendment from the other house takes precedence of a motion to agree or disagree.

A bill originating in one house, is passed by the other with an amendment. The originating house agrees to their amendment with an amendment. The other may agree to their amendment with an amendment; that being only in the 2d and not the 3d degree. For as to the amending house, the first amendment with which they passed the bill, is a part of its text; it is the only text they have agreed to. The amendment to that text by the originating house, therefore, is only in the first degree, and the amendment to that again by the amending house is only in the 2d, to wit, an amendment to an amendment, and so admissible.— Just so when, on a bill from the originating house, the other, at its 2d reading, makes an amendment; on the 3d reading, this amendment is become the text of the bill, and if an amendment to it be moved, an amendment to that amendment may also be moved, as being only in the 2d degree.

Another example

SEC. XLVI.
CONFERENCES.

IT is on the occasion of amendments between the houses that conferences are usually asked; but they may be asked in all cases of difference of opinion between the two houses on matters depending between them. The request of a conference however must always be by the house which is possessed of the papers. 3 *Hats.* 31. 1 *Grey*, 425.

Conferences may be simple or free

Conferences may be either simple or free. At a conference simply, written reasons are prepared by the house asking it, and they are read and delivered, without debate, to the managers of the other house at the conference; but are not then to be answered. 3 *Grey*, 144. The other house then, if satisfied, vote the reasons satisfactory, or say nothing; if not satisfied, they resolve them not satisfactory, and ask a conference on the subject of the last conference, where they read and deliver in like manner written answers to those reasons. 3 *Grey*, 183. They are meant chiefly to record the justification of each house to the nation at large, and to posterity, and in proof that the miscarriage of a necessary measure is not imputable to them. 3 *Grey* 255. At free conferences, the managers discuss viva voce and freely, and interchange propositions for such modifications as may be made in a parliamentary way, and may bring the sense of the two houses together. And each party reports in writing to their respective houses, the substance of what is said on both sides, and it is entered in their journals. 9 *Grey*, 220. 3 *Hats.* 280. This report cannot be amended or altered, as that of a committee may be. *Journ. Sen. May 24, 1796.*

Free conferences

A conference may be asked before the house asking it has come to a resolution of disagreement, insisting or adhering. 3 *Hats.* 269. 341. In which case the papers are not left with the other conferees, but are brought back to be the foundation of the vote to be given. And this is the most reasonable and respectful proceeding. For, as was urged by the Lords on a particular occasion, 'it is held vain and below the wisdom of parliament to reason or argue against fixed resolutions, and upon terms of impossibility to persuade.' 3 *Hats.* 226. So the Commons say 'an adherence is never delivered at a free conference, which implies debate.' 10 *Grey*, 147. And on another occasion the Lords made it an objection that the Commons had asked a free conference after they had made resolutions of adhering. It was then affirmed however on the part of

THOMAS JEFFERSON

the Commons, that nothing was more parliamentary than to proceed with free conferences after adhering. 3 *Hats*. 269, and we
do in fact see instances of conference, or of
free conference, asked after the resolution
of disagreeing. 3 *Hats*. 251. 253. 260. 286.
291. 316. 349. of insisting, *ib*. 280. 296. 299.
319. 322. 355. of adhering, 269. 270. 283.
300; and even of a second or final adherence. 3 *Hats*. 270. And in all cases of conference asked after a vote of disagreement,
&c. the conferees of the house asking it are
to leave the papers with the conferees of
the other: and in one case where they refused to receive them, they were left on the
table in the conference chamber. *Ib*. 271.
317. 323. 354. 10 *Grey*, 146.

After a free conference, the usage is to
proceed with free conferences, and not to return
again to a conference. 3 *Hats*. 270. 9 *Grey*, 229.

After a conference denied, a free conference may be asked. 1 *Grey*, 45.

Subject of conference must be expressed

When a conference is asked, the subject of it must be expressed, or the conference
not agreed to; *Ord. H. Commons* 89. 1 *Grey*,
425. 7 *Grey*, 31. They are sometimes asked to
enquire concerning an offence or default of a
member of the other house. 6 *Grey*, 181. 1
Chandler, 304. Or the failure of the other house

to present to the king a bill passed by both
houses. 8 *Grey*, 302. Or on information received,
and relating to the safety of the nation. 10 *Grey*,
171. Or when the methods of parliament are
thought by the one house to have been departed
from by the other, a conference is asked to come
to a right understanding thereon. 10 *Grey*, 148. So
when an unparliamentary message has been
sent, instead of answering it, they ask a conference. 3 *Grey*, 155. Formerly, an address, or
articles of impeachment, or a bill with
amendments, or a voice of the house, or concurrence in a vote, or a message from the
king, were sometimes communicated by way
of conference. 6 *Grey*, 128. 300. 387. 7 *Grey*, 80.
8 *Grey*, 210. 255. 1 *Torbuck's deb.* 278. 10 *Grey*,
293. 1 *Chandler* 49, 287. But this is not the
modern practice. 8 *Grey*, 255.

    A conference has been asked after the
first reading of a bill. 1 *Grey*, 194. This is a
singular instance.

Some
reasons for
conferences

SEC. XLVII.
MESSAGES.

MESSAGES between the houses are to be
sent only while both houses are sitting. 3 *Hats.*
15. They are received during a debate, without adjourning the debate. 3 *Hats.* 22.

In Senate the messengers are introduced in any state of business, except, 1. While a question is putting. 2. While the Yeas and Nays are calling. 3. While the ballots are calling. The 1st case is short: the 2d and 3d are cases where any interruption might occasion errors difficult to be corrected. So arranged June 15, 1798.

The Speaker of the House

In the House of Representatives, as in Parliament, if the House be in committee when a messenger attends, the Speaker takes the chair to receive the message, and then quits it to return into committee, without any question or interruption. 4 *Grey,* 226.

Messengers are not saluted by the members, but by the Speaker for the house. 2 *Grey,* 253. 274.

Correcting errors

If messengers commit an error in delivering their message, they may be admitted, or called in, to correct their message. 4 *Grey,* 41. Accordingly, March 13, 1800, the Senate having made two amendments to a bill from the House of Representatives, their Secretary, by mistake, delivered one only; which being inadmissible by itself, that house disagreed, and notified the Senate of their disagreement. This produced a discovery of the mistake. The secretary was sent to the other House to correct his mistake, the correction was received, and the two amendments acted on de novo.

As soon as the messenger, who has brought bills from the other house, has retired, the Speaker holds the bill in his hand, and acquaints the House 'that the other House have, by their messenger, sent certain bills,' and then reads their titles, and delivers them to the clerk to be safely kept, till they shall be called for to be read. *Hak.* 178.

It is not the usage for one house to inform the other by what numbers a bill has passed. 10 *Grey* 150. Yet they have sometimes recommended a bill, as of great importance to the consideration of the house to which it is sent. 3 *Hats.* 25. Nor when they have rejected a bill from the other house, do they give notice of it; but it passes sub silentio, to prevent unbecoming altercations. 1 *Blackst.* 183.

But in Congress the rejection is notified by message to the house in which the bill originated.

A question is never asked by the one house of the other by way of message, but only at a conference; for this is an interrogatory, not a message. 3 *Grey*, 151. 181.

When a bill is sent by one house to the other, and is neglected, they may send a message to remind them of it. 3 *Hats.* 25. 5

Grey, 154. But if it be mere inattention, it is better to have it done informally, by communications between the Speakers, or members of the two houses.

English customs　　Where the subject of a message is of a nature that it can properly be communicated to both houses of parliament, it is expected that this communication should be made to both on the same day. But where a message was accompanied with an original declaration, signed by the party to which the message referred, its being sent to one house was not noticed by the other, because the declaration, being original, could not possibly be sent to both houses at the same time. 2 *Hats.* 260. 261. 262.

The king, having sent original letters to the Commons, afterwards desires they may be returned, that he may communicate them to the Lords. 1 *Chandler*, 303.

SEC. XLVIII.
ASSENT.

THE house which has received a bill and passed it may present it for the king's assent, and ought to do it, though they have not by message notified to the other, their passage of it. Yet the notifying by message is a form which ought to be observed between the two houses from motives of respect, and good understanding. 2 *Hats.* 242. Were the bill to be withheld from being presented to the king, it would be an infringement of the rules of parliament. *ib.*

When a bill has passed both houses of Congress, the house last acting on it, notifies its passage to the other, and delivers the bill to the joint committee of enrollment, who see that it is truly enrolled in parchment. When the bill is enrolled, it is not to be written in paragraphs, but solidly and all of a piece, that the blanks between the paragraphs may not give room for forgery. 9 *Grey*, 143. *It is then put into the hands of the clerk of the House of Representatives to have it signed by the Speaker. The clerk then brings it by way of message to the Senate to be signed by their President. The secretary of the Senate returns it to the committee of enrollment, who present it to the President of the United States. If he approves, he signs and deposits it among the rolls in the office of the secretary of state, and notifies by message the Hhouse in which it originated, that he has approved and signed it; of which that house informs the other by message. If the President disapproves, he is to return it, with his objections, to that house in which it shall have originated; who are to enter the objections at large on their journal, and proceed*

Avoiding forgery after a bill has passed

The President's role

Overcoming
the veto of
the President

to reconsider it. *If after such reconsideration, two thirds of that house shall agree to pass the bill, it shall be sent, together with the President's objections, to the other house, by which it shall likewise be reconsidered; and if approved by two thirds of that house, it shall become a law. If any bill shall not be returned by the President within ten days (Sunday excepted) after it shall have been presented to him, the same shall be a law, in like manner as if he had signed it, unless the Congress, by their adjournment, prevent its return; in which case it shall not be a law.* Constitution United States, I. 7.

     Every order, resolution, or vote, to which the concurrence of the Senate and house of Representatives may be necessary, (except on a question of adjournment) shall be presented to the President of the United States, and before the same shall take effect, shall be approved by him, or being disapproved by him, shall be repassed by two thirds of the Senate and house of Representatives, according to the rules and limitations prescribed in the case of a bill. Constitution United States, I. 7.

SEC. XLIX.
JOURNALS.

EACH house shall keep a journal of its proceedings, and from time to time publish the same, excepting such parts as may, in their judgment, require secrecy. Constitution I. 5.

Every vote of Senate shall be entered on the journals, and a brief statement of the contents of each petition, memorial or paper, presented to the Senate, be also inserted on the journals. Rule 24.

The proceedings of the Senate, when not acting as in a committee of the house, shall be entered on the journals, as concisely as possible, care being taken to detail a true account of the proceedings. Rule 26.

The titles of bills, and such parts thereof only as shall be affected by proposed amendments, shall be inserted on the journals. Rule 27.

If a question is interrupted by a vote to adjourn, or to proceed to the orders of the day, the original question is never printed in the journal, it never having been a vote, nor introductory to any vote: but when suppressed by the Previous Question, the first question must be stated, in order to introduce and make intelligible the second. 2 *Hats.* 83.

So also when a question is postponed, adjourned, or laid on the table, the original question, though not yet a vote, must be expressed in the journals; because it makes part of the vote of postponement, adjourning, or laying it on the table.

The Congressional Record

THOMAS JEFFERSON

Where amendments are made to a question, those amendments are not printed in the journals, separated from the question; but only the question as finally agreed to by the house. The rule of entering in the journals only what the house has agreed to, is founded in great prudence and good sense; as there may be many questions proposed which it may be improper to publish to the world, in the form in which they are made. 2 *Hats.* 85.

Recording votes

In both houses of Congress all questions whereon the Yeas and Nays are desired by one fifth of the members present, whether decided affirmatively or negatively, must be entered in the journals. Constitution I. 5.

The first order for printing the votes of the house of Commons was October 30, 1685. 1 *Chandler* 387.

Some judges have been of opinion, that the journals of the house of Commons are no records, but only remembrances. But this is not law. *Hob.* 110. 111. *Lex. parl.* 114. 115. *Journ. H. C. Mar.* 17, 1592. *Hale parl.* 105. For the Lords in their house have power of judicature, the Commons in their house have power of judicature, and both houses together have power of judicature; and the book of the clerk of the House of Commons is a record, as is affirmed by act of parliament, 6 H. 8. *c.* 16. 4 *Inst.* 23. 24. and every member of the House of Commons hath a judicial place. 4 *Inst.* 15. As records, they are open to every person, and a printed vote of either house is sufficient ground for the other to notice it. Either may appoint a committee to inspect the journals of the other, and report what has been done by the other in any particular case. 2 *Hats.* 261. 3 *Hats.* 27—30. Every member has a right to see the journals, and to take and publish votes from them. Being a record, every one may see and publish them. 6 *Grey*, 118. 119.

On information of a misentry or omission of an entry in the Journal, a committee may be appointed to examine and rectify it, and report it to the House. 2 *Hats,* 194. 5.

Correcting errors

SEC. L.
ADJOURNMENT.

THE two houses of parliament have the sole, separate, and independent power of adjourning each their respective houses. The king has no authority to adjourn them; he can only signify his desire, and it is in the wisdom and prudence of either house to comply with his requisition, or not, as they see fitting. 2 *Hats.* 232. 1 *Blackstone*, 186. 5 *Grey*, 122.

Consent necessary for adjournment

By the Constitution of the United States, a smaller number than a majority may adjourn from day to day. I. 5. *But 'neither house, during the session of Congress, shall, without the consent of the other, adjourn for more than three days, nor to any other place than that in which the two houses shall be sitting.'* I. 5. *And in case of disagreement between them with respect to the time of adjournment, the President may adjourn them to such time as he shall think proper.* Constitution II. 3.

A motion to adjourn simply, cannot be amended as by adding 'to a particular day.' But must be put simply 'that this house do now adjourn?' and if carried in the affirmative, it is adjourned to the next sitting day, unless it has come to a previous resolution 'that at its rising it will adjourn to a particular day,' and then the House is adjourned to that day. 2. *Hats.* 82.

Where it is convenient that the business of the house be suspended for a short time, as for a conference presently to be held, &c. it adjourns during pleasure. 2. *Hats.* 305. Or for a quarter of an hour. 5. *Grey.* 331.

If a question be put for adjournment, it is no adjournment till the Speaker pronounces it. 5. *Grey.* 137. And from courtesy and respect, no member leaves his place till the Speaker has passed on.

SEC. LI.
A SESSION.

PARLIAMENT have three modes of separation, to wit, by adjournment, by prorogation, or dissolution by the king, or by the efflux of the term for which they were elected. Prorogation or dissolution constitutes there what is called a session, provided some act has passed. In this case all matters depending before them are discontinued, and at their next meeting are to be taken up de novo, if taken up at all. 1 *Blackst.* 186. Adjournment, which is by themselves, is no more than a continuance of the session from one day to another, or for a fortnight, a month, &c. ad libitum. All matters depending remain in statu quo, and when they meet again, be the term ever so distant, are resumed without any fresh commencement, at the point at which they were left. 1 *Lev.* 165. *Lex. Parl.* c. 2. 1 *Ro. Rep.* 29. 4 *Inst.* 7. 27. 28. *Hutt.* 61. 1 *Mod.*

Defining a session

252. *Ruffh. Jac's. L. Dict. Parliament.* 1 *Blackst.* 186. Their whole session is considered in law but as one day, and has relation to the first day thereof. *Bro. abr. parliament.* 86.

Committees may be appointed to sit during a recess by adjournment, but not by prorogation. 5 *Grey,* 374. 9 *Grey,* 350. 1 *Chandler,* 50. Neither house can continue any portion of itself in any parliamentary function beyond the end of the session, without the consent of the other two branches. When done, it is by a bill constituting them commissioners for the particular purpose.

How Congress can adjourn

Congress separate in two ways only, to wit, by adjournment, or dissolution by the efflux of their time. What then constitutes a session with them? A dissolution certainly closes one session, and the meeting of the new Congress begins another. The constitution authorises the President 'on extraordinary occasions, to convene both houses or either of them.' I. 3. If convened by the President's proclamation, this must begin a new session, and of course determine the preceding one to have been a session. So if it meets under the clause of the constitution which says, 'the Congress shall assemble at least once in every year, and such meeting shall be on the first

Monday in December, unless they shall by law appoint a different day.' I. 4. This must begin a new session. For even if the last adjournment was to this day, the act of adjournment is merged in the higher authority of the constitution, and the meeting will be under that, and not under their adjournment. So far we have fixed land marks for determining sessions. In other cases, it is declared by the joint vote authorising the President of the Senate and the Speaker to close the session on a fixed day, which is usually in the following form, "Resolved by the Senate and house of Representatives, that the President of the Senate and the Speaker of the house of Representatives be authorised to close the present session by adjourning their respective houses on the —day of—.'

When it was said above, that all matters depending before parliament were discontinued by the determination of the session, it was not meant for judiciary cases, depending before the House of Lords, such as impeachments, appeals, and writs of error. These stand continued of course, to the next session. *Raym.* 120. 381. *Ruffh. Jac. L. D. Parliament.*

Impeachments stand in like manner continued before the Senate of the United States.

SEC. LII.
TREATIES.

*The President
and the
Senate*

THE *President of the United States has power, by and with the advice and consent of the Senate, to make treaties, provided two thirds of the Senators present concur.* Constitution United States II. 2.

    Resolved that all confidential communications, made by the President of the United States to the Senate, shall be, by the members thereof, kept inviolably secret; and that all treaties, which may hereafter be laid before the Senate shall also be kept secret until the Senate shall, by their resolution, take off the injunction of secrecy. December 22, 1800.

    Treaties are legislative acts. A treaty is a law of the land. It differs from other laws only as it must have the consent of a foreign nation, being but a contract with respect to that nation. In all countries, I believe, except England, treaties are made by the legislative power: and there also, if they touch the laws of the land, they must be approved by Parliament. *Ware v. Hylton.* 3. *Dallas Rep.* 273. It is acknowledged, for instance, that the King of Great Britain cannot by a treaty make a citizen of an alien. *Vattel. B.* 1. *c.* 19. *sec.* 214. An act of parliament was necessary to validate the American treaty of 1783. And abundant examples of such acts can be cited. In the case of the treaty of Utretcht in 1712, the commercial articles required the concurrence of parliament. But a bill brought in for that purpose was rejected. France, the other contracting party, suffered these articles, in practice, to be not insisted on, and adhered to the rest of the treaty. 4. *Russel's Hist. Mod. Europe* 457. 2. *Smollet.* 242. 246.

By the Constitution of the United States this department of legislation is confided to two branches only of the ordinary legislature; the President originating, and the Senate having a negative. To what subjects this power extends, has not been defined in detail by the constitution; nor are we entirely agreed among ourselves. 1. It is admitted that it must concern the foreign nation party to the contract, or it would be a mere nullity, res inter alios acta. 2. By the general power to make treaties, the constitution must have intended to comprehend only those subjects which are usually regulated by treaty, and cannot be otherwise regulated. 3. It must have meant to except out of these the rights reserved to the states; for surely the President and Senate cannot do by treaty what the whole government is interdicted from doing in any way. 4. And also to except those subjects of legislation in which it gave a partici-

The President originates; the Senate agrees or disagrees

pation to the house of Representatives. This last exception is denied by some on the ground that it would leave very little matter for the treaty power to work on. The less the better, say others. The constitution thought it wise to restrain the Executive and Senate from entangling and embroiling our affairs with those of Europe. Besides, as the negociations are carried on by the Executive alone, the subjecting to the ratification of the Representatives such articles as are within their participation is no more inconvenient than to the Senate. But the ground of this exception is denied as unfounded. For examine, e.g. the treaty of commerce with France, and it will be found that out of 31 articles, there are not more than small portions of two or three of them which would not still remain as subjects of treaties, untouched by these exceptions.

Revoking treaties

Treaties being declared, equally with the laws of the United States, to be the supreme law of the land, it is understood that an act of the legislature alone can declare them infringed and rescinded. This was accordingly the process adopted in the case of France in 1798.

Ratification

It has been the usage for the Executive, when it communicates a treaty to the Senate for their ratification, to communicate also the correspondence of the negotiators. This having been omitted in the case of the Prussian treaty, was asked by a vote of the house of February 12, 1800, and was obtained. And in December 1800, the convention of that year between the United States and France, with the report of the negociations by the envoys, but not their instructions, being laid before the Senate, the instructions were asked for and communicated by the President.

The mode of voting on questions of ratifications is by nominal call.

Resolved, as a standing rule, that whenever a treaty shall be laid before the Senate for ratification, it shall be read a first time for information only; when no motion to reject, ratify or modify the whole or any part shall be received.

That its second reading shall be for consideration; and on a subsequent day, when it shall be taken up as in a committee of the whole, and every one shall be free to move a question on any particular article in this form, "Will the Senate advise and consent to the ratification of this article?" or to propose amendments thereto, either by inserting or by leaving out words, in which last case the question shall be, "Shall the words stand part of the article?" And in every of the said cases, the concurrence of two-thirds of the Senators present shall be requisite to decide affirmatively. And when, through the whole, the proceedings shall be stated to the house, and questions be again severally put thereon for confirmation, or new ones proposed, requiring in like manner a concurrence

Advise and Consent

of two-thirds for whatever is retained or inserted.

That the votes so confirmed shall, by the house, or a committee thereof, be reduced into the form of a ratification with or without modifications, as may have been decided, and shall be proposed on a subsequent day, when every one shall again be free to move amendments, either by inserting or leaving out words; in which last case the question shall be, "Shall the words stand part of the resolution?" And in both cases the concurrence of two-thirds shall be requisite to carry the affirmative; as well as on the final question to advise and consent to the ratfication in the form agreed to. Rule of January 6, 1801.

Resolved, that when any question may have been decided by the Senate in which two-thirds of the members present are necessary to carry the affirmative, any member who voted on that side which prevailed in the question, may be at liberty to move for a reconsideration: and a motion for reconsideration shall be decided by a majority of votes. Rule of February 3, 1801.

SEC. LIII.
IMPEACHMENT.

The role of each house

THE *House of Representatives shall have the sole power of impeachment.* Constitution United States, I. 3.

The Senate shall have the sole power to try all impeachments. When sitting for that purpose, they shall be on oath or affirmation. When the President of the United States is tried, the chief justice shall preside: and no person shall be convicted without the concurrence of two-thirds of the members present. Judgment in cases of impeachment shall not extend further than to removal from office, and disqualification to hold and enjoy any office of honor, trust, or profit under the United States. But the party convicted shall nevertheless be liable and subject to indictment, trial, judgment and punishment, according to law. Constitution, I. 3.

The President, Vice-President, and all civil officers of the United States, shall be removed from office on impeachment for, and conviction of treason, bribery, or other high crimes and misdemeanors. Constitution, II. 4.

The trial of crimes except in cases of impeachment shall be by jury. Constitution, III. 2.

These are the provisions of the Constitution of the United States on the subject of impeachments. The following is a sketch of some of the principles and practices of England on the same subject.

Jurisdiction. The lords cannot impeach any to themselves, nor join in the accusation, because they are the judges. *Seld.*

Who can be impeached

British practices and customs

Impeachment

Judic. in Parl. 12, 63. Nor can they proceed against a Commoner but on complaint of the Commons. *id.* 84. The lords may not, by the law, try a commoner for a capital offence, on the information of the king, or a private person; because the accused is entitled to a trial by his peers generally; but on accusation by the House of Commons, they may proceed against the delinquent of whatsoever degree, and whatsoever be the nature of the offence; for there they do not assume to themselves trial at common law. The Commons are then instead of a jury, and the judgment is given on their demand, which is instead of a verdict. So the Lords do only judge, but not try the delinquent. *id.* 6. 7. But Wooddeson denies that a Commoner can now be charged capitally before the Lords, even by the commons; and cites Fitzharris's case, 1681, impeached of high treason, where the Lords remitted the prosecution to the inferior court. 8 *Grey's deb.* 325—7. 2 *Wooddeson*, 601. 576. 3 *Seld.* 1610. 1619. 1641. 4 *Blacks.* 257. 3 *Seld.* 1604. 1618. 9. 1656.

Accusation. The commons, as the grand inquest of the nation, become suitors for penal justice. 2 *Woodd.* 597. 6 *Grey* 356. The general course is to pass a resolution containing a criminal charge against the supposed delinquent, and then to direct some member to impeach him by oral accusation, at the bar of the House of Lords, in the name of the Commons. The person signifies that the articles will be exhibited, and desires that the delinquent may be sequestered from his seat, or be committed, or that the peers will take order for his appearance. *Sachev. trial.* 325. 2 *Wood.* 602, 605. *Lords. Journ.* 3 *June* 1701. 1 *Wms.* 616. 6 *Grey* 324.

Trial by a jury of peers

Process. If the party do not appear, Proclamations are to be issued, giving him a day to appear. On their return they are strictly examined. If any error be found in them, a new Proclamation issues, giving a short day. If he appear not, his goods may be arrested, and they may proceed. *Seld. Jud.* 98. 99.

Articles. The accusation (articles) of the Commons is substituted in place of an indictment. Thus, by the usage of parliament, in impeachment for writing or speaking, the particular words need not be specified. *Sach. tr.* 325. 2 *Wood.* 602—605. *Lords Journ.* 3 *June,* 1701. 1 *Wms.* 616.

Appearance. If he appears, and the case be capital, he answers in custody: though not if the accusation be general. He is not to be committed but on special accusations. If it be for a misdemeanor only, he answers, a lord

Personal defense

in his place, a commoner at the bar, and not in custody, unless, on the answer, the Lords find cause to commit him, till he finds sureties to attend, and lest he should fly. *Seld. Jud.* 98. 99. A copy of the articles is given him, and a day fixed for his answer. *T. Ray.* 1 *Rushw.* 268. *Fost.* 232. 1 *Clar. Hist. of the Reb.* 379. On a misdemeanor, his appearance may be in person, or he may answer in writing, or by attorney. *Seld. Jud.* 100. The general rule on an accusation for a misdemeanor is that in such a state of liberty or restraint as the party is when the Commons complain of him, in such he is to answer. *id.* 101. If previously committed by the Commons, he answers as a prisoner. But this may be called in some sort judicium parium suorum. *ib.* In misdemeanors the party has a right to counsel by the common law; but not in capital cases. *Seld. Jud.* 102—5.

Answer. The answer need not observe great strictness of form. He may plead guilty, as to part, and defend as to the residue; or, saving all exceptions, deny the whole, or give a particular answer to each article separately. 1 *Rush.* 274. 2 *Rush.* 1374. 12 *Parl. hist.* 442. 3 *Lords Journ.* 13 *Nov.* 1643. 2 *Woodd.* 607. But he cannot plead a pardon in bar to the impeachment. 2 *Wood.* 615. 2 *St. tr.* 735.

Replication, Rejoinder, &c. There may be a replication, rejoinder, &c. *Seld. Jud.* 114. 8 *Grey's deb.* 233. *Sachev. tr.* 15. *Journ. H. of Commons*, 6 *March*, 1640. 1.

Witnesses. The practice is to swear the witnesses in open house, and then examine them there: or a committee may be named, who shall examine them in committee, either on interrogatories agreed on in the house, or such as the committee in their discretion shall demand. *Seld. Jud.* 120. 123.

Jury. In the case of Alice Pierce, 1 *R.* 2. a jury was impanelled for her trial before a committee. *Seld. Jud.* 123. But this was on a complaint, not on impeachment by the Commons. *Seld. Jud.* 163. It must also have been for a misdemeanor only, as the Lords spiritual sat in the case, which they do on misdemeanors, but not in capital cases. *id.* 148. The judgment was a forfeiture of all her lands and goods. *id.* 188. This, Selden says, is the only jury he finds recorded in parliament for misdemeanors: but he makes no doubt, if the delinquent doth put himself on the trial of his country, a jury ought to be impanelled, and he adds that it is not so on impeachment by the commons; for they are in loco proprio, and there no jury ought to be empanelled. *id.* 124. The Ld. Berkeley, 6 *E.* 3. was arraigned

Trial by a jury of one's peers

Judgment under the law

for the murder of, *L.* 2. on an information on the part of the king, and not on impeachment of the Commons; for then they had been patria sua. He waived his peerage, and was tried by a jury of Gloucestershire and Warwickshire. *id.* 125. In 1 *H.* 7. the Commons protest that they are not to be considered as parties to any judgment given, or hereafter to be given in parliament. *id.* 133. They have been generally, and more justly, considered, as is before stated, as the grand jury. For the conceit of Selden is certainly not accurate, that they are the patria sua of the accused, and that the Lords do only judge, but not try. It is undeniable that they do try. For they examine witnesses as to the facts, and acquit or condemn, according to their own belief of them. And Lord Hale says, 'the peers are judges of law as well as of fact.' 2 *Hale P. C.* 275. Consequently of fact as well as of law.

Presence of Commons. The Commons are to be present at the examination of witnesses. *Seld. Jud.* 124. Indeed they are to attend throughout, either as a committee of the whole house, or otherwise, at discretion, appoint managers to conduct the proofs. *Rushw. tr. of Straff,* 37. *Com. Journ.* 4 *Feb.* 1709. 10. 2 *Woodd.* 614. And judgment is not to be given till they demand it. *Seld. Jud.* 124. But they are not to be present on impeachment when the Lords consider of the answer or proofs, and determine of their judgment. Their presence however is necessary at the answer and judgment in cases capital, *id.* 158, 159, as well as not capital. 162. The Lords debate the judgment among themselves. Then the vote is first taken on the question of guilty or not guilty: and if they convict, the question, or particular sentence is out of that which seemeth to be most generally agreed on. *Seld. Jud.* 167. 2 *Woodd.* 612.

Judgment. Judgments in parliament for death have been strictly guided per legem terrae, which they cannot alter: and not at all according to their discretion. They can neither omit any part of the legal judgment, nor add to it. Their sentence must be secundum, non ultra legem. *Seld. Jud.* 168—171. This trial, though it varies in external ceremony, yet differs not in essentials from criminal prosecutions before inferior courts. The same rules of evidence, the same legal notions of crimes and punishments prevail. For impeachments are not framed to alter the law, but to carry it into more effectual execution against too powerful delinquents. The judgment therefore is to be such as is warranted by legal

Sentencing according to the law

principles or precedents. 6 *Sta. tr.* 14. 2 *Woodd.* 611. The chancellor gives judgments in misdemeanors; the Lord High Steward formerly in cases of life and death. *Seld. Jud.* 180. But now the Steward is deemed not necessary. *Fost.* 144. 2 *Woodd.* 613. In misdemeanors the greatest corporal punishment hath been imprisonment. *Seld. Jud.* 184. The king's assent is necessary in capital judgments, (but 2 *Woodd.* 614. contra) but not in misdemeanors. *Seld. Jud.* 136.

Continuance. An impeachment is not discontinued by the dissolution of parliament: but may be resumed by the new parliament. *T. Ray.* 383. 4 *Com. Journ.* 23 *Dec.* 1790. *Lords Jour. May* 16, 1791. 2 *Woodd.* 618.

THE END.

INDEX

143

COSIMO is a specialty publisher of books and publications that inspire, inform and engage readers. Our mission is to offer unique books to niche audiences around the world.

COSIMO CLASSICS offers a collection of distinctive titles by the great authors and thinkers throughout the ages. At **COSIMO CLASSICS** timeless classics find a new life as affordable books, covering a variety of subjects including: *Biographies, Business, History, Mythology, Personal Development, Philosophy, Religion and Spirituality,* and much more!

COSIMO-on-DEMAND publishes books and publications for innovative authors, non-profit organizations and businesses. **COSIMO-on-DEMAND** specializes in bringing books back into print, publishing new books quickly and effectively, and making these publications available to readers around the world.

COSIMO REPORTS publishes public reports that affect your world: from global trends to the economy, and from health to geo-politics.

FOR MORE INFORMATION CONTACT US AT
INFO@COSIMOBOOKS.COM

❈ If you are a book-lover interested in our current catalog of books.

❈ If you are an author who wants to get published

❈ If you represent an organization or business seeking to reach your members, donors or customers with your own books and publications

COSIMO BOOKS ARE ALWAYS AVAILABLE AT ONLINE BOOKSTORES

——— VISIT COSIMOBOOKS.COM ———
BE INSPIRED, BE INFORMED

CPSIA information can be obtained at www.ICGtesting.com
232704LV00001B/63/A

9 781602 061033